Ralf Habel

Real-time Rendering and Animation of Vegetation

Ralf Habel

Real-time Rendering and Animation of Vegetation

Advances in displaying vegetation for interactive applications

Südwestdeutscher Verlag für Hochschulschriften

Impressum/Imprint (nur für Deutschland/ only for Germany)
Bibliografische Information der Deutschen Nationalbibliothek: Die Deutsche Nationalbibliothek
verzeichnet diese Publikation in der Deutschen Nationalbibliografie; detaillierte bibliografische
Daten sind im Internet über http://dnb.d-nb.de abrufbar.
Alle in diesem Buch genannten Marken und Produktnamen unterliegen warenzeichen-, marken-
oder patentrechtlichem Schutz bzw. sind Warenzeichen oder eingetragene Warenzeichen der
jeweiligen Inhaber. Die Wiedergabe von Marken, Produktnamen, Gebrauchsnamen,
Handelsnamen, Warenbezeichnungen u.s.w. in diesem Werk berechtigt auch ohne besondere
Kennzeichnung nicht zu der Annahme, dass solche Namen im Sinne der Warenzeichen- und
Markenschutzgesetzgebung als frei zu betrachten wären und daher von jedermann benutzt
werden dürften.

Verlag: Südwestdeutscher Verlag für Hochschulschriften Aktiengesellschaft & Co. KG
Dudweiler Landstr. 99, 66123 Saarbrücken, Deutschland
Telefon +49 681 37 20 271-1, Telefax +49 681 37 20 271-0, Email: info@svh-verlag.de
Zugl.: Vienna, Vienna University of Technology, Diss., 2009

Herstellung in Deutschland:
Schaltungsdienst Lange o.H.G., Berlin
Books on Demand GmbH, Norderstedt
Reha GmbH, Saarbrücken
Amazon Distribution GmbH, Leipzig
ISBN: 978-3-8381-0499-7

Imprint (only for USA, GB)
Bibliographic information published by the Deutsche Nationalbibliothek: The Deutsche
Nationalbibliothek lists this publication in the Deutsche Nationalbibliografie; detailed
bibliographic data are available in the Internet at http://dnb.d-nb.de.
Any brand names and product names mentioned in this book are subject to trademark, brand or
patent protection and are trademarks or registered trademarks of their respective holders. The
use of brand names, product names, common names, trade names, product descriptions etc.
even without a particular marking in this works is in no way to be construed to mean that such
names may be regarded as unrestricted in respect of trademark and brand protection legislation
and could thus be used by anyone.

Publisher:
Südwestdeutscher Verlag für Hochschulschriften Aktiengesellschaft & Co. KG
Dudweiler Landstr. 99, 66123 Saarbrücken, Germany
Phone +49 681 37 20 271-1, Fax +49 681 37 20 271-0, Email: info@svh-verlag.de

Copyright © 2009 by the author and Südwestdeutscher Verlag für Hochschulschriften
Aktiengesellschaft & Co. KG and licensors
All rights reserved. Saarbrücken 2009

Printed in the U.S.A.
Printed in the U.K. by (see last page)
ISBN: 978-3-8381-0499-7

Dedicated to my mother,
Elsbeth Habel.

Abstract

Vegetation rendering and animation in real-time applications still pose a significant problem due to the inherent complexity of plants. Both the high geometric complexity and intricate light transport require specialized techniques to achieve high-quality rendering of vegetation in real time. This thesis presents new algorithms that address various areas of both vegetation rendering and animation.

For grass rendering, an efficient algorithm to display dense and short grass is introduced. In contrast to previous methods, the new approach is based on ray tracing to avoid the massive overdraw of billboard or explicit geometry representation techniques, achieving independence of the complexity of the grass without losing the visual characteristics of grass such as parallax and occlusion effects as the viewpoint moves.

Also, a method to efficiently render leaves is introduced. Leaves exhibit a complex light transport behavior due to subsurface scattering and special attention is given to the translucency of leaves, an integral part of leaf shading. The light transport through a leaf is precomputed and can be easily evaluated at runtime, making it possible to shade a massive amount of leaves while including the effects that occur due to the leaf structure such as varying albedo and thickness variations or self shadowing.

To animate a tree, a novel deformation method based on a structural mechanics model that incorporates the important physical properties of branches is introduced. This model does not require the branches to be segmented by joints as other methods, achieving smooth and accurate bending, and can be executed fully on a GPU. To drive this deformation, an optimized spectral approach that also incorporates the physical properties of branches is used. This allows animating a highly detailed tree with thousands of branches and ten thousands of leaves efficiently.

Additionally, a method to use dynamic skylight models in spherical harmonics precomputed radiance transfer techniques is introduced, allowing to change the skylight parameters in real time at no considerable cost and memory footprint.

Acknowledgements

This thesis would not have been possible without the support of many people. First, I would like to thank Prof. Werner Purgathofer for the excellent work infrastructure of the Institute of Computer Graphics and Algorithms. Also, I would like to thank Michael Wimmer, my thesis advisor, for the input and helpful discussions. I also would like to thank my co-author Alexander Kusternig for the energetic and competent support with the implementations.

Thanks goes to my collegues Stefan Jeschke, Oliver Mattausch, Matthias Bernhard and Daniel Scherzer who provided valuable input and inspiring sessions at the white board. The students Bogdan Mustata and Thomas Gamper also contributed to the implementations and brain storming. I am also indebted for the very useful comments of Peter-Pike Sloan from the Graphics Research Group at Microsoft.

Furthermore, I would like to thank the Institute of Computer Aided Automation for providing the 3D scanning and lighting equipment to generate the leaf data sets. Finally, I want to thank my parents and my brother for supporting me throughout the creation of this thesis.

Contents

Abstract	i
Acknowledgements	iii
1 Introduction	**1**
1.1 Motivation	1
1.2 Challenges	2
1.3 Dissertation Thesis	3
1.4 Contributions	4
2 Grass Rendering	**7**
2.1 Introduction	7
2.2 State of the Art	7
2.2.1 Volumetric and Shell-Based Grass	9
2.2.2 BTF based grass	10
2.2.3 Level-of-Detail Methods	13
2.3 Ray Tracing Grass	15
2.3.1 Grid Ray Tracer	18
2.3.2 Grass Animation	23
2.3.3 Results	24
2.3.4 Summary	26
3 Leaf Rendering	**29**
3.1 Introduction	29
3.2 State of the Art	30
3.2.1 Measurements	31
3.2.2 Radiative Transfer Models	32
3.2.3 Diffusion-Based Models	34
3.3 A Leaf Model for Real-Time Rendering	36
3.3.1 Overview	37
3.3.2 Data Acquisition	37
3.3.3 Reflectance	41

CONTENTS

		3.3.4	Translucency	42
		3.3.5	Light Diffusion in Leaves	44
		3.3.6	Light diffusion as an image convolution process	46
		3.3.7	Real-Time Translucency	49
		3.3.8	The Half Life 2 Basis	50
		3.3.9	Projecting Translucency into the HL2 basis	53
		3.3.10	Results	55
		3.3.11	Summary	59

4 Physically Guided Animation of Trees — 61
- 4.1 Introduction — 61
- 4.2 State of the Art — 61
  - 4.2.1 Structural Elements — 62
  - 4.2.2 Animation — 63
- 4.3 Hierarchical Vertex Displacement — 67
- 4.4 Beam Model — 69
  - 4.4.1 Euler-Bernoulli Beam Model — 69
  - 4.4.2 Length Correction — 72
  - 4.4.3 Branch Deformation — 74
- 4.5 Synthesizing Branch Motion — 76
  - 4.5.1 Turbulent Wind and Motion — 76
  - 4.5.2 Stochastic Motion Synthesis — 77
  - 4.5.3 2D Motion Textures — 78
  - 4.5.4 Wind Direction — 81
- 4.6 Applying Beam Deformation and Branch Motion — 82
- 4.7 Leaves — 83
  - 4.7.1 Leaf Deformation — 83
  - 4.7.2 Leaf Animation — 84
- 4.8 Results — 85
- 4.9 Summary — 87

5 Skylight Models for SH-Lighting — 89
- 5.1 Introduction — 89
- 5.2 Related Work — 90
  - 5.2.1 Spherical Harmonics Lighting — 91
  - 5.2.2 Preetham Skylight Model — 91
- 5.3 Dynamic Skylight — 92
  - 5.3.1 Polynomial Fitting and Reconstruction — 93
  - 5.3.2 Error Measurement — 94
  - 5.3.3 Gibbs Phenomenon Suppression — 94
- 5.4 Results — 96

5.5 **Summary** 97

6 **Summary and Conclusions**   **101**
  6.1 **Key Contributions** 101
  6.2 **Research Outlook** 103
  6.3 **Conclusion** 104

Appendix A   **105**

List of Figures   **107**

List of Tables   **110**

Bibliography   **113**

*Of all the wonders of nature,
a tree in summer is perhaps the most remarkable;
with the possible exception of a moose singing
"Embraceable You" in spats.*

Woody Allen

1
Introduction

The field of computer graphics, i.e. the science of creating images and animations synthetically, has a remarkable speed in its technological advances. Its applications are ubiquitous in modern technology, ranging from mobile devices to computer games and movies, from medical applications to virtual reality.

A more specific area of computer graphics, the field of real-time graphics, is concerned with the interactive creation of images, allowing a user to navigate or edit the contents interactively. Being interactive requires the calculations to fulfill strong constraints, the image needs to be created in about 16 milliseconds. To some extent, it is already possible to create photorealistic applications within this constraint, though highly specialized and sophisticated techniques and preprocesses have to be used.

The calculation power of hardware dedicated to create pictures interactively doubles about every year, exceeding Moore's Law and allowing for more and more complex calculations to create realistic images interactively. A modern hardware has the same power as a supercomputer a decade ago, leveraging the possibility to parallelize the required calculations.

Of course, computer games are the main driving force behind this development, but other applications also start to use the capabilities and possibilities of a GPU[1] to its full extent. Most modern computers are equipped with a capable GPU, allowing the mainstream user to use applications with sophisticated rendering techniques.

1.1 Motivation

Vegetation in all its different forms is almost always part of a scenery, be it fully natural or urban. Even in completely cultivated areas or indoor scenes, though not very dominant, potted plants or alley trees and patches of grass

---
[1] Graphics Processing Unit

are usually part of a surrounding. With computer graphics simulating the real world, it is no surprise that vegetation has been an essential and wide ranging research area in computer graphics since the beginning.

Vegetation in computer graphics can be roughly categorized into the field of modeling the growth of a plant by generating its geometry, and the field of modeling the appearance and behavior of plants in an environment. Though real plants all basically use the same processes to grow, a plethora of methods can be applied to generate plants at various ages, ranging from fractals [71], L-Systems [79] and procedural approaches [24] to full simulations of ecosystems [27], among others. To display and to animate this generated geometry interactively, specialized representations, lighting and shading techniques together with animation or simulation methods are applied to incorporate the non-geometric attributes of vegetation. Of course, both fields are strongly connected since the environment impacts the growth of a plant [43]. Also, geometric representation and lighting or shading techniques are heavily dependent on each other since geometric attributes need to be transported by the representation in order to have them available for shading.

Though the generation of plants has received more attention than other aspects of vegetation, only the combination of accurate geometry, appearance and dynamic behavior results in a convincing result. Especially under real-time conditions, all facets of displaying vegetation pose significant problems, which makes interactive rendering and animation of vegetation one of the biggest challenges in real-time graphics. In this thesis, we want to face this challenge and provide solutions for a number of open problems.

1.2 Challenges

The term vegetation is a broad term, covering structures such as lawns up to complete landscapes covered with a forest. Rendering vegetation is substantially different from rendering geometry with less geometric complexity such as houses, manufactured products or other objects consisting of largely connected surfaces.

Many computer games and virtual reality applications are already very realistic, though most lack a realistic display of plants and trees due to their inherent complexity. Especially for trees and grass, many standard acceleration and simplification methods cannot be applied. This results in severe compromises in the realism of their appearance compared to other parts of a scene. There are several reasons why vegetation is more difficult to display than other objects:

Geometric Complexity A lawn or meadow for example consists of millions of small grass blades and a full geometric representation is, due to both memory and calculation time constraints, not feasible, and simpler representations are needed. The goal is to still be able to render and animate grass that looks convincing and volumetric in its appearance by keeping the important visual properties of grass.

Concerning trees and treelike plants, it is possible to use a full geometry representation on current hardware, though only a limited amount of polygons can be spent on each branch and leaf depending on the corresponding size and shape, also limiting the number of branches to a few thousand and the number of leaves to a few ten thousand.

A tree in full geometry representation poses challenges to create realistic animations under the given real-time constraint since every branch and leaf is perceived as a separate part and thus needs to be treated separately. The structure of a tree consists of a complex hierarchy of branches to which leaves are attached, all of which interact with a turbulent wind field, and every part of the tree must react consistently to wind in order to achieve a realistic and convincing animation of a complete tree.

Light Interaction Vegetation is not only complex in geometry, also the light interaction of leaves or grass blades is highly intricate. A leaf for example usually consists of different layers and is strongly structured, which has a profound impact on both the reflectance and translucency of leaves, an integral part of the light interaction of vegetation. Additionally, many leaves differ not only between species but also in their light transport on the front and back, depending on the nature of the surface, and no general assumptions can be made.

Natural Lighting To display realistic vegetation, care must be taken not only about the geometry and light interaction, but also about the overall lighting conditions in natural scenes. The subtle influences of a skylight need to be incorporated in addition to the sun's contribution into the calculations in order to create convincing renderings of natural outdoor scenes.

1.3 Dissertation Thesis

This work focuses on some specific parts of this huge problem set, which requires specialized techniques for different situations and plant species.

The main thesis of this work is that it is possible to render and animate vegetation in real time by designing algorithms that fully execute on the

CHAPTER 1. INTRODUCTION

GPU, using its parallel processing power. This way, highly detailed effects in all aspects of displaying vegetation can be calculated efficiently.

1.4 Contributions

A variety of new approaches and improvements over existing techniques is presented in this thesis. They are mainly concerned with rendering and animation of grass and trees, though a more general improvement for skylight lighting for spherical harmonics precomputed radiance transfer is also introduced, which may be used to achieve realistic vegetation lighting.

Grass Rendering and Animation   To render short and dense grass efficiently, a technique that uses front-to-back compositing of implicitly defined grass slices is presented. To achieve that, the slices are ray traced in the fragment shader, leveraging the parallel power of a GPU, which allows easy integration into existing frameworks. Front-to-back compositing significantly reduces the overhead and overdraw associated with common vegetation rendering systems. The technique also does not require geometric specifications of the grass since grass is treated as a volumetric grid over a carrier polygon.

A texture-based approach to animate the grass combines global wind movements with local turbulences to emulate the highly complex interaction of grass with turbulent wind, creating a convincing animation. These results have been published in

- Ralf Habel, Michael Wimmer and Stefan Jeschke, **Instant Animated Grass**. In Václav Skala, editor in chief, *Journal of WSCG* 2007, 15 1–3, pages 123–128, ISBN 978-80-86943-00-8

Leaf Rendering   A new shading model for real-time rendering of plant leaves that reproduces all important attributes of leaves is shown. It allows for a large number of leaves to be shaded since the model can be instanced over the complete plant. In particular, a physically based model for accurate subsurface scattering on the translucent side of directly lit leaves is introduced. A preprocess formulated as an image convolution is used and the result is expressed in an efficient directional basis (Half-Life 2 Basis) that is fast to evaluate. Additionally, a data acquisition method for leaves that uses off-the-shelf devices is shown. The results of this work have been published in

1.4. CONTRIBUTIONS

- Ralf Habel, Alexander Kusternig and Michael Wimmer, **Physically Based Real-Time Translucency for Leaves**. In Jan Kautz and Sumanta Pattanaik, editors, *Rendering Techniques 2007 (Proceedings Eurographics Symposium on Rendering)* 2007, pages 253–263, ISBN 978-3-905673-52-4

Tree Animation A new method to animate the interaction of a tree with wind in real time is presented. It combines statistical observations with physical properties in two major parts of tree animation. The deformation resulting from the forces of wind is approximated by a novel efficient two step nonlinear deformation method, allowing arbitrary continuous deformations and circumventing the need to segment a branch to model its deformation behavior.

To animate the deformation, the interaction of wind with the dynamic system representing a tree is stochastically modeled. The response functions of branches to turbulent wind are precomputed in frequency space, allowing to synthesize the branch motions efficiently by sampling a 2D motion texture.

The combination of both methods can be implemented inside a vertex shader using only the GPU and allows animating thousands of branches and ten thousands of leaves at practically no cost. This work has been published in

- Ralf Habel, Alexander Kusternig and Michael Wimmer, **Physically Guided Animation of Trees**. In P. Dutre and M. Stamminger, editors, *Computer Graphics Forum (Proceedings Eurographics 2009)*, 28(2)

Spherical Harmonics Lighting with the Preetham Skylight Model
A fast and compact representation of a skylight model for spherical harmonics precomputed radiance transfer lighting is shown. This representation allows dynamically changing the parameters of the skylight model on a per frame basis. The method is applied to the Preetham skylight model since this model can deliver both realistic colors and dynamic range and is the most used model in real-time graphics. The parameters are separated in its spherical harmonics extension and a polynomial two-dimensional linear least squares fit for the principal parameters is performed to avoid any significant memory and computation costs. To remove ringing, a domain specific Gibbs phenomena suppression is executed before used for precomputed radiance transfer. The results of this research have been published in

CHAPTER 1. INTRODUCTION

- Ralf Habel, Bogdan Mustata and Michael Wimmer, **Efficient Spherical Harmonics Lighting with the Preetham Skylight Model**. In Katerina Mania and Erik Reinhard, editors, *Eurographics 2008 - Short Papers* 2008, pages 119–122, ISSN 1017-4656

In creating, the only hard thing is to begin:
a grass blade's no easier to make than an oak.
　　　　　　James Russell Lowell

2

Grass Rendering

2.1 Introduction

Interactive rendering of vegetation plays an important role in virtual reality and computer games where grass is an essential part of most natural scenes. Unfortunately, grass is also very complex. Modeling each grass blade individually in a landscape would require a huge amount of geometry, making a naive geometric approach impractical for interactive rendering. Also, quite different kinds of grass exist, ranging from short mowed grass areas such as football fields to high growing meadows in forest scenes.

To render grass efficiently, acceleration techniques and different representations of the grass geometry have to be applied, simplifying the rendering process while still keeping the appearance of grass. A plethora of very different approaches can be applied, depending on the grass properties as well as relative position to the camera or other attributes. Usually, different methods are mixed to cover the full range from close-up views to complete terrain viewpoints in order to optimize the quality to performance ratio. In Section 2.2, different approaches to grass rendering are presented. Additionally, their advantages and disadvantages are shown while in Section 2.3, the novel ray tracing based approach to rendering grass is given.

2.2 State of the Art

Image-based Rendering (IBR) is in general the most common approach for vegetation since geometry that is too complex to render can be well approximated by IBR techniques. By far, the most widely used and simplest IBR approach displaying grass is to use semitransparent textured billboards. These are instanced over the ground to create individual tufts or completely covered grass areas, using different configurations of billboards such as star shaped quadrilaterals or long stripes fitted to the terrain. This technique,

CHAPTER 2. GRASS RENDERING

with different optimizations, is used by virtually every commercial virtual reality application or computer game. Usually, not only grass but the complete vegetation is represented through billboards and billboard clouds. Even the most advanced games still use billboards to represent vegetation as can be seen in the game Crysis [3](see Figure 2.1). The big advantage of us-

Figure 2.1: A screenshot of the game Crysis using billboards for vegetation rendering. (picture: [3])

ing billboards is that they do not require any changes or special care in the rendering pipeline. They only use the standard methods of triangle-based geometry and textures, and can be combined with standard shading algorithms such as different lighting models or shadow techniques. Also, billboards pose few restrictions as to what kinds of plants can be represented, making them a versatile technique for practical vegetation rendering. They can also be animated by standard approaches such as vertex displacement [73, 47].

However, this approximation comes at a cost since billboards make heavy use of transparency. In a meadow for example, the depth complexity is very high since it cannot be decided if or which part of a billboard is visible in a frame and the billboards need to be rendered back-to-front. This causes a tremendous amount of overdraw and therefore limits the amount of billboards that can be used. This problem can be somewhat diminished by depth sorting, but usually a large amount of billboards are used, all of which need to be sorted on a frame-by-frame basis if the camera moves over the grass.

This allows rendering grass in a front-to-back order but does not allow the billboards to intersect.

Another drawback is that the quality of appearance is limited, especially at viewpoints close to the grass. The fact that flat surfaces are used becomes salient, and the lack of proper parallax and occlusion destroys the realistic appearance. Nonetheless, a simple billboard representation can be considered the most successful basic technique and is consequently used in more advanced methods as a level of detail.

2.2.1 Volumetric and Shell-Based Grass

Grass shares a lot of attributes with fur. Since both structures are dense, semi-volumetric and consist of thread-like primitives, similar approaches can be taken. To display such volumetric effects, Kajiya and Kay [51] introduced volumetric textures, called "texels". In this context, texels are representations of a three-dimensional material by a cubic reference volume that is mapped onto a surface repeatedly. A texel itself is a three-dimensional array approximating the visual properties of a micro-surface. They were created to solve the problem of spatial aliasing when ray-tracing complex geometries. An extension of volumetric textures and their application to natural scenes was presented by Neyret [67]. Grass rendered with this approach can bee seen in Figure 2.2. Unfortunately, rendering a texel involves front-to-back compositing along a ray in a dense volumetric texture, which makes their use in real-time graphics very limited.

Rendering The typical real-time implementation of texels uses stacks of polygons, mapped with semi-transparent textures [10, 9, 56, 55, 63]. In shell-based approaches, copies of the base terrain mesh are created by displacing the vertices along the normals as seen in Figure 2.3. This is best done by providing enough duplicate vertices and performing the displacement directly in the vertex shader. The shells are then mapped with a semitransparent texture where the opaque parts are at the cross sections of the grass blades. As proposed by Bakay et al. [9], the height can be encoded in the alpha channel and only one texture is needed to map all shells. By rendering the shells in bottom to top order and blending the results, fur or grass can be rendered similar to the fully volumetric approach. However, slices that are parallel to a terrain geometry are not optimal for viewing positions typical for walkthroughs, with objectionable artifacts at viewpoints close to the grass and at grazing angles (see Figure 2.3). Shell-based techniques are rather suitable for viewing from above such as in a flight simulator. Also, the complexity of the grass that can be displayed is limited to very isotropic

CHAPTER 2. GRASS RENDERING

Figure 2.2: Grass ray traced through volumetric texels. (picture: [67])

and straight grass since the approach does not use any method based on photographic textures. Features that break the isotropy such as flowers or tufts are hard to integrate with this approach. Additionally, many shells are required to gain the appearance of vertical structures from horizontal shells and to suppress visual artifacts. A terrain textured with shell-based grass is shown in Figure 2.4. However, shell-based techniques are very successful in rendering fur where high density and isotropy is inherent.

Animation An advantage of shell-based approaches is that the grass can be easily animated by modulating the vertices. Neyret et al. [67] for example apply a force field to animate the vertices of the extruded shells. Care must be taken to avoid stretching, which can be counteracted by additionally modulating the height of the extruded vertices as shown by Bakay et al. [9]. Also, more elaborate wind models and simulations such as spring mass models can be applied without modification [10].

2.2.2 BTF based grass

A more general method, Bidirectional Texture Functions (BTF) [23, 64], can be applied to rendering grass. A BTF is a 6-dimensional function depending

2.2. STATE OF THE ART

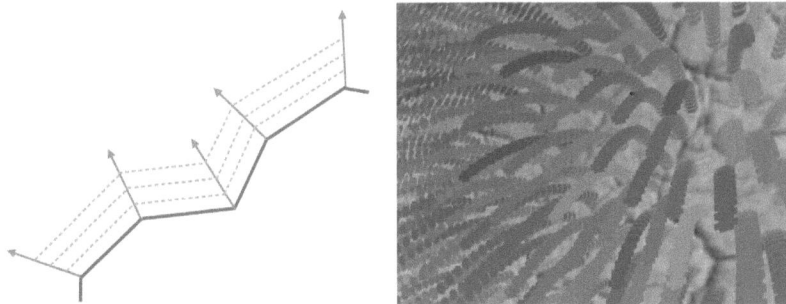

Figure 2.3: Shells over a terrain and the resulting grass. (pictures: [9])

Figure 2.4: Terrain with shell based grass. (picture: [10])

on planar texture coordinates as well as on view and illumination spherical angles. This function can be acquired by a set of images of a material sample taken with different camera and light positions. Due to the high dimensionality of the function, several thousand images have to be created to express high-frequency lighting changes. This also limits the practical resolution and compression schemes have to be applied in order to make this approach practical for real-time graphics.

Rendering As proposed by Shah et al. [86], the BTF of a grass patch can be created synthetically by using an offline renderer where complex light interactions such as global illumination can be included. The BTF does not

CHAPTER 2. GRASS RENDERING

include any depth information since the spatial dimensions only cover the texture coordinates. In order to render silhouettes and proper occlusion with objects intersecting the grass, a separate function that only encodes the depth as a function of the camera angle is used. To compress the BTF, Shah et.al use Principal Component Analysis (PCA) and only encode the chromaticity, since the grass is assumed to be of general uniform color. This simplification allows using only the first five eigenvectors to sufficiently reconstruct the original color information.

At runtime, the BTF is evaluated with the lighting transformed in local tangent space. To produce the result for arbitrary camera and light directions, the three closest sampled directions are used. To achieve correct silhouette and intersection, the correct z-buffer values are also reconstructed, which has been generated at a higher resolution than the BTF to avoid depth aliasing. A complete terrain can be covered by simply tiling the BTF and blending the borders to decrease tiling artifacts. A terrain shaded with this method can be seen in Figure 2.5.

Figure 2.5: BTF based grass. (pictures: [86])

A disadvantage of this approach is that a BTF-based approach is limited by memory, which does not allow a high-resolution BTF and due to the necessary tiling, variations in appearance are strongly limited. Also, an expensive decompression on a per-pixel level is required, thus making this method heavily fill-rate limited. On the other hand, a BTF with depth function is not dependent on the complexity of the represented geometry and lighting solution without sacrificing proper intersection and silhouette rendering, which makes it a good choice for very dense and short grass at a reasonable distance.

Animation The biggest drawback of a BTF based method is that it is not possible to animate the grass, since any spatial correlations of the geometry

2.2. STATE OF THE ART

are lost. One could apply texture coordinate animation, but this would not result in high-quality animation. Though, it may still provide satisfactory movements of grass at far distances.

2.2.3 Level-of-Detail Methods

Up to now, only one kind of grass representation has been used to render grass. Of course, using different representations at different distances to the camera makes it possible to optimize the quality of grass displayed. The two main publications using levels of detail (LOD) are by Perbet et al. [74] and Boulanger et al. [15]. They both use a full geometry representation for the highest LOD and a simple texture map for the lowest LOD. Where they differ is the mid-level LOD and shading and animation methods applied. The main problem that arises in using different LODs is to achieve consistency in shading and animation between different LODs and their transition from one into another, as well as in grass density and general appearance.

Rendering As the highest LOD is a full geometry representation of each grass blade, standard rendering methods are used, though one has to use proper blending if grass blades are textured semitransparently. On this level, shading is important to get a realistic look and due to the high polygon count, standard methods may be prohibitively expensive. To get dynamic lighting and shadowing, Boulanger [15] proposes a fast approximation tailored for grass rendering. For ground shadows, the grass vertices are projected to the ground and rendered into a stencil buffer. To render inter-blade shadows, a cylindrical visibility map which contains the neighboring grass blades is preprocessed (see Figure 2.6). This shadow mask is evaluated with a ray-cylinder intersection of the light direction at runtime.

The mid-level LOD in Perbet et al.[74] consists of the standard approach of billboards. The consistency between full geometry and billboard representation is maintained by precomputing the blades' positions and control points in the texture space of the billboard LOD. The transition is done by rendering and blending the two LODs. Compared to this, Boulanger et al. use a volumetric approach by rendering an axis-aligned 2D vertical grid, mapped with a semitransparent texture as seen in Figure 2.7. Since the used textures are created by rendering the full geometry grass slice by slice, the appearance is consistent. To address the dynamic lighting in this LOD, a form of low-frequency BTF is applied. Textures for both front and back sides of a grass slice with lighting along the three principal axis, both negative and positive directions, are precalculated and blended at runtime according to the dynamic light direction.

CHAPTER 2. GRASS RENDERING

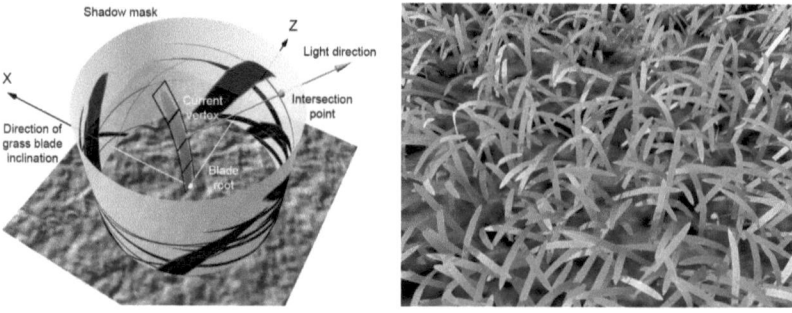

Figure 2.6: Shadow mask of a grass blade (left) and resulting shadows (right). (pictures: [15])

Boulanger et al. also incorporate density mapping to define the density of grass through a map. For the highest LOD, the map simply defines how many grass blades are rendered. To modulate the mid-level LOD, each grass slice has a density threshold map that assigns a threshold to each containing grass slice and allows cutting out grass slices from the calculations to decrease the number of blades displayed in a grass slice. To avoid popping while in transition between different LODs and densities, the result of each LOD is blended in transitional regions. The result of this approach can be seen in Figure 2.8.

Mixing different representations of grass leads to efficient and high-quality renderings since they can be fitted to the current requirements of the viewpoint. A major drawback of a mixed approach is that one has to keep track of all representations within the viewport and blending between them requires using different representations for the same grass patch and therefore requires more intricate implementations. Also, it is not trivial to achieve consistency between LODs, especially if the grass is animated. But depending on the quality of grass required, LOD methods deliver the highest quality for close up views for a relative modest performance hit.

Animation Whereas Boulanger does not propose any form of animation, Perbet [101] applies wind primitives, allowing interaction with the grass and avoiding a full simulation which would require a prohibitive amount of resources for a complete grass covered terrain. The highest LOD is animated by precomputing postures through a physical simulation, and then blended at runtime to create the swaying of the grass. To animate the grass in the mid-level LOD, the vertices are animated, whereas in the transition region, the animation of each grass blade is calculated and the previously mentioned

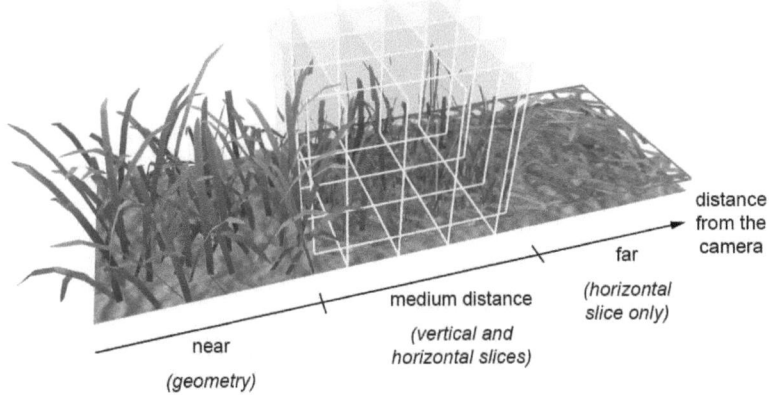

Figure 2.7: Different LODs of grass. (picture: [15])

control points in texture space are used for animation to ensure consistency of animation in transitional regions.

2.3 Ray Tracing Grass

As described, grass can be rendered well in a volumetric approach as shown in Section 2.2.1 or the mid-level LOD of Boulanger (Section 2.2.3). In the volumetric case, partial opacity of the used textures pose a problem since grass is inherently a high-frequency structure and requires proper blending to avoid severe aliasing artifacts.

Typically, a grass texture is fully transparent between the individual grass blades and fully opaque within the blades. However, partial opacity arises at the edges of the grass blades if the grass texture is a filtered version of a higher resolution texture, which is the case for MIP-mapping, or if it has been generated using an anti-aliased renderer in the first place. Therefore, the colors and opacities of billboards overlapping in screen space need to be correctly composited. Just as in volume rendering, this can be done either in back-to-front or front-to-back fashion [54].

Back-to-front compositing corresponds to standard transparency alpha blending used when rendering the billboards as geometry. But back-to-front compositing can be very inefficient because all slices have to be traversed in order to get a correct result. Furthermore, if the billboards intersect each other, a consistent back-to-front order does not exist. The popular alternative of using alpha testing instead of alpha blending leads to noticeable aliasing

CHAPTER 2. GRASS RENDERING

Figure 2.8: Meadow rendered with the method proposed by Boulanger [15].

artifacts especially at the edges of the grass blades, at viewpoints close to the grass.

Front-to-back compositing, on the other hand, is typically used with ray tracing and allows for early ray termination when the accumulated opacity is sufficiently high. This effect can be exploited for grass rendering as well. Instead of rendering the textured grass billboards using polygons, they can be implicitly defined on a carrier polygon and ray traced in the fragment shader using front-to-back compositing (also known as the "over"-operator [77]). The billboards are arranged as a regular vertical 2D or 3D grid, depending on height and quality of the grass. This approach has the advantage to exit the ray traversal and respectively the fragment shader when the opacity reaches a user-defined threshold. Since the billboards are ray traced, the intersecting billboards are handled automatically, always giving correct compositing results. The illusion of grass can be maintained even when executing a small, fixed number of iterations which allows limiting the number of intersections and thus the resources needed.

Therefore, this approach combines the advantages of ray tracing volumetric structures as proposed by Kajiya and Kay [51] with grass rendering, while still being efficient enough for real-time graphics and using current hardware to its full extent.

The setup of the ray tracing step is very similar to relief mapping [76],

2.3. RAY TRACING GRASS

where a height map, defined in a shell carried by polygons, is ray traced in the fragment shader. As with relief mapping, the regular grid of grass billboards therefore seems to reside inside the carrier polygon (see Figure 2.9).

Figure 2.9: A quad patch (wireframe overlay) rendered with fully opaque textures. The grid structure is generated in the fragment shader.

The difference is ray tracing a height field inside the fragment shader can only be done with a search, either through a linear and following recursive search or through other spatial search structures. Arranging the billboards in a regular grid, on the other hand, has the advantage that the intersection can be calculated analytically with the ray-plane intersection equation and no search or corresponding search structure is needed.

Probably the most significant advantage of ray tracing grass in the fragment shader is the ease of modeling and integration into existing rendering systems. The grass is defined as a material rather than geometry, and no

CHAPTER 2. GRASS RENDERING

change to the scene definition is required. Compared to a polygon-based approach, only the carrier polygon has to be given instead of hand-modeled billboards or a fitted polygonal grid.

2.3.1 Grid Ray Tracer

In order to cover a complete terrain with ray traced grass, a dataset that defines a patch of grass is defined using the tangent space (u, v, w) of the carrier polygon. This patch is then instanced all over the terrain. A basic grass patch consists of the ground texture and a texture containing one sub-texture for each billboard (or slice) in the patch. Additionally, a fully opaque grass slice needs to be provided (see Figure 2.10). As the grass textures are

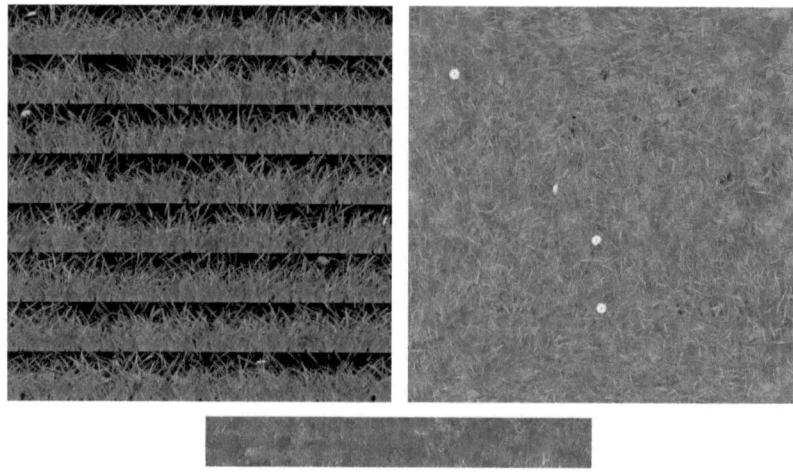

Figure 2.10: A grass data set consisting of grass blades (left), a ground texture (right) and a fully opaque grass slice (bottom).

packed in one texture, a border of at least 1 pixel needs to be incorporated to avoid filtering artifacts. The same set of billboard textures is used for both principal axes of a regular vertical 2D grid. Since they will be applied in an orthogonal fashion, there is no visible repeating pattern. This is just for convenience and consistency of appearance, the number of slices used and how they are applied is not limited by the shown method.

The general approach is depicted in Figure 2.11. The camera view is transformed into tangent space, and a ray is cast from the carrier polygon into the shell. This shell is defined by the carrier polygon at the top and a virtual

2.3. RAY TRACING GRASS

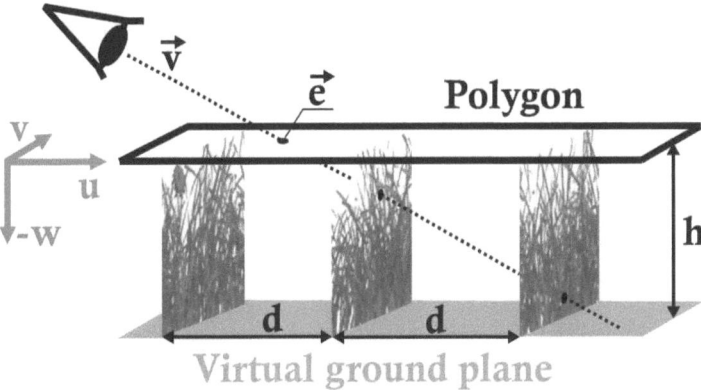

Figure 2.11: A ray is cast from the viewing point through a grid of grass slices.

ground plane at the bottom, which is offset by a user-defined distance along the negative tangent-space w axis at the vertices (i.e., the inverted normal vectors). Then, the intersections with the grid are calculated up to a user defined number of intersections. If there is some remaining transparency in the result, the remainder is filled with the fully opaque grass slice. Because all color blending is performed inside the fragment shader, any form of blending is possible.

In order to save performance, the tangent space vectors are calculated in the vertex shader and interpolated for the fragment shader. Additionally, the view vector $\vec{v}$ in tangent space (interpolated from $\vec{p} - \vec{s}$ at each vertex $\vec{p}$ and viewpoint $\vec{s}$), and the interpolated texture coordinates (which give the ray entry point $\vec{e}$, see Figure 2.11) are passed from the vertex shader.

The user also has to provide the parameters $d_{u,v}$ for the distance between the slices in tangent space and the depth of the ground plane h. Those values should approximate the image ratios of the used grass slice textures to avoid strong stretching of the textures as they are mapped to the billboards. d_u and d_v do not necessarily have to be the same, but the isotropy of the grass is greatly improved by choosing them to be the same value. The billboards are aligned to the tangent space axes, so a billboard can be simply represented by a scalar. With these given values the shader executes the following steps:

1. Set entry point $\vec{e}$ with interpolated texture coordinates.

2. Calculate for both u and v a texture offset to select the initial grass slices.

CHAPTER 2. GRASS RENDERING

3. Adjust this offset depending on the sign of the view vector so the same slice is seen from both sides.

4. Calculate the positions $p_{u,v}$ of the first planes to be ray traced in both u and v directions according to $d_{u,v}$ using a `floor()` operator.

5. Enter the ray tracing loop.

Before entering the ray tracing loop in item 2, two parameters need to be set for both the u and v axis. Depending on the sign of the viewing vector in u and v, a texture offset to address different grass slices and a correction parameter are calculated. They assure that the same grass slice is seen from both sides and that there are no inconsistencies in the texture lookups during the ray casting.

Following this setup, the inner ray tracing loop consists of the following steps:

1. Calculate the intersections with the next slice in u and v direction. Since the slices are axis aligned, the ray-plane intersection

$$\vec{x} = \vec{e} + \vec{v} \cdot \frac{\vec{n}_p \cdot (\vec{p} - \vec{e})}{\vec{n}_p \cdot \vec{v}}, \tag{2.1}$$

where $\vec{n}_p$ is the normal vector and $\vec{p}$ is an arbitrary point on the plane, simplifies to

$$\vec{x} = \vec{e} + \vec{v} \cdot \frac{p_{u,v,w} - e_{u,v,w}}{v_{u,v,w}}, \tag{2.2}$$

depending on which axis is used.

2. Choose the closer intersection point and increment (or decrement, depending on the sign of v) the corresponding billboard by $d_{u,v}$.

3. Test intersection point against the virtual ground polygon. If the intersection is outside the shell, intersect the ray with the ground polygon using equation 2.2.

4. Composit the current color $\vec{c}$ with the color of the slice $\vec{c}_i$ (with associated alpha values α and α_i) using the standard "over" blending function, assuming that colors are premultiplied with their corresponding opacity values:

$$\begin{aligned} \vec{c} &= \vec{c} + (1-\alpha) \cdot \vec{c}_i \\ \alpha &= \alpha + (1-\alpha) \cdot \alpha_i \end{aligned} \tag{2.3}$$

2.3. RAY TRACING GRASS

After the ray tracing loop, the remaining transparency is filled with a texture lookup from the fully opaque grass slice or the average color of the grass data set. A single grass patch rendered with the data set of Figure 2.10 using 16 slices for both u and v axes can be seen in Figure 2.12. A very low number (4 was used in the images shown) of ray casting iterations is already sufficient for high image quality, also limiting the number of required texture reads. On some modern GPUs, it may prove better to exit the ray casting loop as

Figure 2.12: A quad patch rendered with the data set of Figure 2.10. The grid structure is apparent at perpendicular angles but vanishes at more grazing angles.

soon as a pixel is fully opaque. Depending on the hardware used and the dataset used, an early loop exit should be considered because many pixels are fully opaque after one or two ray tracing steps, and this may result in a considerable speedup.

If the grid structure is too apparent, which is mostly the case if the grass is seen primarily from a perpendicular angle and for high grass, an additional horizontal plane at half of the shells' depth can avoid this artifact. The ray casting step is simply extended by this vertical analogue to the ground plane. As can be seen in Figure 2.13, the grid structure vanishes even at perpendicular viewing angles.

CHAPTER 2. GRASS RENDERING

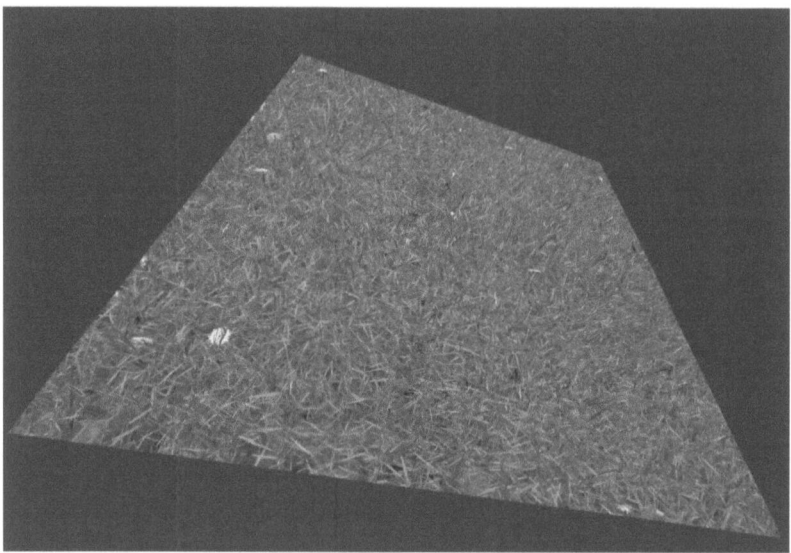

Figure 2.13: A quad patch with the same data set as in Figure 2.12, but with an additional horizontal plane at half the ground depth. The grid structure is not dominant even at perpendicular angles.

Visibility Interactions Up to now, only the proper color is calculated while the depth is calculated as the depth of the carrier polygon. If an object is inside the grass, it will be clipped at the carrier polygon. A correct depth value of the grass needs to be calculated in order to resolve the visibility of objects in the grass. The clipping effect compared to correct visibility is shown in Figure 2.14. The fully correct solution would be to render all opaque objects first and generate an offscreen buffer with the corresponding depth information (e.g. using multiple render targets). While rendering the grass, the depth value at which to terminate a ray can be read from this buffer. The drawback is that this method requires a non-trivial modification of the rendering pipeline as multiple passes are needed. Another, simpler solution is to generate the depth value while ray casting inside the fragment shader and set the depth as an output value. The depth value is extracted when a user-specified threshold of opacity has been reached during the ray casting loop. Since the ray casting is done in tangent space, the calculated depth of a ray has to be transformed into camera space and added to the depth of the carrier polygon. This approach does not require any modification of the rendering pipeline and gives correct occlusion for the fully opaque parts of the

2.3. RAY TRACING GRASS

Figure 2.14: A grass patch with (left) and without (right) correct visibility.

grass blades. The drawback is that the semi-transparent parts of grass are not handled exactly, but the artifacts introduced are unnoticeable in practice due to the high frequency structure of the grass.

2.3.2 Grass Animation

As with any grass rendering technique, the overall realism of grass depends greatly on wether it is animated or not. Even the simplest techniques such as animating the vertices of a polygonal billboard with simple periodic functions increase the quality considerably since the scene is not perceived as static. Because ray traced grass is texture based, a more sophisticated approach can be applied that is also texture based. A realistic simulation of grass movement has to take two components into account. On the one hand, gusts of wind cause relatively large areas of grass to bend in the same direction. On the other hand, high-frequency wind turbulences near the ground cause smaller, but more random movements of grass blades.

Since there are no vertices defined that could be animated, the animation is done by distorting the texture lookups, which also allows one to increase the applied spatial frequencies up to the size of a texel. A horizontal shear transformation per texture lookup of the grass billboards is performed, resulting in a distortion along the u or v direction, depending on the billboard's orientation in tangent space. This offset is looked up from a tileable noise map that is mapped over the complete terrain. To avoid repetitive animation, this noise map should cover several grass patches. To achieve the shear transformation, the offset is linearly scaled with the height of the animated texel above the virtual ground plane which can be calculated from the ray-plane intersection. This way, the grass stays fixed on the ground and the distortion increases linearly to the top of a billboard to mimic the complex movements of grass in wind. To animate the grass in time, the noise map is translated over the terrain along the wind direction.

It may seem that, because the transformation executed is a shear transformation, the imposed stretching may be objectionable. Fortunately, only small perturbations are needed to animate the grass. Also, every grass blade performs a different shearing, which distracts from the stretching due to the complexity of the movements. This animation method can also be used to animate polygonal billboards and is used in a modified and extended form by Sousa et al. [93] for example.

The advantage of texture-based animation is that any procedural or hand-crafted texture can be used as long as the texture is tileable. For the shown pictures, the noise texture was created by using a low-frequency and a high-frequency Perlin noise function [75]. The low-frequency noise function with a high amplitude emulates gusts of wind while the high-frequency function with lower amplitudes emulates the erratic movements caused by small turbulences of grass blades. A more sophisticated way to create the texture is to use spectral methods as proposed by Stam [95], defining amplitudes in frequency space and creating the texture through an inverse Fourier transform. An extended form of this approach is also used in the animation of trees in Chapter 4.

2.3.3 Results

The overall performance of the algorithm depends on the number of pixels covered, as one ray is cast per pixel, and the ray-casting depth, defining the number of intersection iterations. The shown screenshots where rendered with an iteration depth of 4, which is already enough to avoid visible artifacts and to display correct visibility of intersecting geometry. The datasets used were generated using Maya and its PaintFX feature, which can deliver highly detailed vegetation geometry. A fully geometric representation was generated, and slices of grass were rendered into textures.

Figure 2.15 shows a terrain covered with 8×8 grass patches, where each patch contains 16 billboards in u and v direction. Another dataset is shown in Figure 2.16, consisting of patches with 32 billboards per direction. An implementation using DirectX 9 and the OGRE [1] open source graphics engine was tested on two different platforms. The full source code of an

2.3. RAY TRACING GRASS

Figure 2.15: A terrain textured with animated grass with moderate grass density and height.

HLSL implementation is shown in Appendix A. A Pentium 4 and a GeForce 7900 GT representing commodity hardware and a modern setup consisting of a Pentium Quad Core at 2.6 GHz and a Geforce 280GTX were used to benchmark the method. The example scene is rendered at a resolution of 1024 × 768 on both systems and additionally at 1600 × 1200 on the Geforce 280GTX to measure the performance under the demands of currently used resolutions in computer games.

To compare these results with standard techniques, the grass in a similar scene was modeled by hand-placed billboards in the same configuration and density as the ray traced grid and standard alpha blending. Compared to this polygonal implementation, the shown method incorporates correct alpha blending and texture based animation. The average frames per second of ray traced grass and the corresponding polygonal representation including the speedup factor is shown in Table 2.1.

As can bee seen, ray tracing grass can deliver a considerable speedup of up to a factor of 2.6 depending on the used hardware, while delivering correct alpha blending. The speedup can be explained by the avoidance of massive

CHAPTER 2. GRASS RENDERING

Figure 2.16: A terrain textured with short, dense grass.

	ray traced fps	polygonal fps	speedup
GeForce 7900GT@1024	140	90	1.5
Geforce 280GTX@1024	640	240	2.6
Geforce 280GTX@1600	290	150	1.9

Table 2.1: Average frames per second for different hardware ans resolutions.

overdraw and the fact that current hardware is fill-rate optimized.

2.3.4 Summary

Besides the considerable speedup, the biggest advantage of ray tracing grass in the pixel shader is that it does not require additional geometry, treating grass as a volumetric material rather than geometry. Any geometry-based grass is limited by the number of polygons that can be used whereas in comparison, the performance of ray traced grass is independent of the density of the billboards, so a massive amount of billboards can be rendered without compromising on important effects such as parallax and correct occlusion of individual grass blades. Additionally, this approach solves the problem of

2.3. RAY TRACING GRASS

compositing in a natural way and can be animated effortlessly. Also, this way rendering grass is confined to a shader which is easily integrable into existing rendering frameworks as shown with the OGRE graphics engine. Further, any standard lighting technique such as light mapping, shadow mapping or normal mapping can be combined with the shown method since the technique is completely texture based. Also, irregular tiling methods such as Wang tiling [21] can be used to map the grass onto a terrain.

However, there are also some drawbacks. If very sparse grass is to be rendered, the iteration depth needs to be much higher than 4 and most intersections do not contribute to the shading of the grass. Though on modern hardware, a higher iteration depth can be chosen since the grass will still render at very high frame rates, the resources are not used optimally. Also, since the ray casting is done in tangent space, the grass can not be rendered with correct silhouettes, which is usually not a problem with low grass, but is a strongly visible artifact when high grass is displayed. This can be avoided by adapting higher order surface approximations as shown by Policarpo et al. [70] for height field-traced surfaces. As with height field-traced surfaces, the camera can not move below the carrier polygon, which limits the height of the grass. This can be avoided by using a full polygonal grass representation as a highest level of detail, switching to ray traced grass as the second LOD analogue to Boulanger et al. [15].

Considering those drawbacks, ray traced grass is best applied to short dense grass such as a football field or a mowed lawn to leverage the advantages of the shown technique while avoiding potential artifacts.

Autumn is a second spring when every leaf is a flower.
   Albert Camus

3
Leaf Rendering

3.1 Introduction

The rendering of leaves in commercial applications such as games and virtual reality simulations is usually avoided completely by representing trees as billboards or billboard clouds. This means that there are no separate leaves and the textures used for the billboard are rendered with standard methods, not taking care of special attributes of leaves. This can already produce somewhat good results if the textures are generated so they benefit the appearance of leaves [53]. But this approach does not reproduce the behavior of leaves in light and can therefore provide only very limited realistic results.

Leaves have a very complex interaction with light and only few assumptions can be made since there is a large variety of leaves. They differ not only in shape and color, but also in surface attributes, ranging from highly glossy surfaces due to thick wax layers to completely diffuse surfaces due to micro hairs. Also, leaves usually show very different light interactions on the adaxial and abaxial side. But the most defining attribute of leaves differentiating them from other surfaces is their translucency, which becomes very apparent in direct sunlight when seen from the unlit side (see Figure 3.1).

Another research area where light-leaf interaction is important is remote sensing, which is usually done by satellite or radar. In order to derive values such as vegetation covering of a landscape, health of plants, water containment of plants, etc., from measurements, accurate models of reflectance, translucency and general light transport inside plants or canopies are required to extrapolate such data. Though those models are targeted to derive biophysical and agricultural properties, they can also be applied to computer graphics. An extensive overview of optical properties in the context of remote sensing can be found in [96].

A realistic leaf can not be modeled using standard methods due to the intricate light-leaf interaction, and specialized methods have to be applied to render convincing vegetation since an important part of the appearance

CHAPTER 3. LEAF RENDERING

Figure 3.1: Leaves in sunlight.

is dominated by the scattering of light inside a leaf. Real-time graphics only tries to model the appearance of objects so fully accurate models that predict the light transport are not required and using measured data to reproduce the appearance without an exact knowledge of the internals is sufficient to display highly realistic results.

In Section 3.3, a novel model for leaf translucency for real-time rendering is presented. It reproduces all important attributes on a physical basis while the model is still able to be instanced in order to display a massive amount of leaves efficiently.

3.2 State of the Art

Scattering of light is a wide field in computer graphics, ranging from scattering in gaseous structures such as clouds or fog to scattering in fluid and solid material such as milk, marble, skin or leaves. In fluid and solid materials which reside inside a non-scattering medium, usually air, the scattering can be described with a BSSRDF [1][68]. Compared to a BSDF [2], the incident

---
[1]Bidirectional Scattering Surface Reflectance Distribution Function
[2]Bidirectional Scattering Distribution Function

light can be at a different position than the exitant light, making a BSSRDF an 8-dimensional nonlocal function. This high dimensionality poses a computational problem which can only be solved exactly by path tracing. Practical methods reduce the dimensionality, compromising on the accuracy of the solution or deriving analytical expressions for special cases.

Concerning real-time rendering, subsurface scattering is an active research area with many results. Examples are skin subsurface scattering [32], scattering in more general lighting conditions [100] or deformable models [62]. Although this field can be seen as a complete sub-area of real-time rendering, only a few publications propose techniques that specifically deal with realistic leaf rendering.

Many properties of a leaf such as local thickness, optical density or internal structure have an essential impact on its appearance. These values are usually not generated synthetically but measured, so data sets have to be created that a model can be fitted or verified to. In the following, different measurement procedures are shown which are then used in different approaches to the problem.

3.2.1 Measurements

As shown in Section 2.2.2, the very general approach to reproduce a surface by measuring or creating a BTF [23, 64] is also a possibility to render leaves. However, the structure of a leaf is not homogeneous due to the vein structure and varying surface properties, which requires the corresponding texture maps to be of high resolution so that a leaf BTF has to be created in its entirety, making this approach impractical for real-time rendering due to the massive memory and high reconstruction costs.

To capture the optical properties of leaves, spectro-photo-goniometers are used, which directly measure the bidirectional reflectance and transmittance [98][16]. These measurements only provide averages over a larger area of a leaf and do not incorporate any spatial variances, but are measured spectrally in both near infrared and optical wavelengths since remote sensing requires accurate spectral resolution rather than spatial resolution. The results can be used to fit standard BRDF and BSDF models in order to be useful to computer graphics [16]. Of course, a BSDF is not sufficient to model a realistic leaf since there is no spatial information which can capture the variations in albedo or surface structures. Photographed textures can be used to modulate the parameters of a BSDF, but in this way, scattering is not correctly accounted for.

To capture the optical properties spatially, Wang et al. [99] propose to use a linear light source (LLS) [37] as seen in Figure 3.2, which enables one

CHAPTER 3. LEAF RENDERING

to estimate the diffuse color, specular color, specular roughness and surface normal on a per-pixel basis. A LLS has the advantage that it can provide

Figure 3.2: A linear light source (LLS) used to measure reflectometry. (picture: [37])

high-resolution maps of all important surface parameters, and is therefore well fit to produce the data needed for realistically rendering leaves. The problem is that the availability of a LLS is limited, and needs to be custom built for this purpose.

3.2.2 Radiative Transfer Models

Many researchers proposed techniques to model subsurface scattering in leaves. One of the first publications that tackle the general problem of SSS and also apply it to leaves is Hanrahan et al. [44]. It uses one-dimensional linear transport theory to derive explicit formulae for reflectance and transmittance. Multiple layers are incorporated and the light transport is modeled with Monte Carlo ray tracing to evaluate the BDFs.

A brute-force approach was applied by Govaerts et al. [41], who represented the internal structure of leaf tissue and the corresponding optical properties explicitly and solved the radiative transfer through ray tracing. A model that is also based on ray tracing but uses available biological information was proposed by Baranoski et al. [11]. It was later extended by precomputing the reflectance and transmittance values that are applied to a

3.2. STATE OF THE ART

simplified scattering model [12]. This model is controlled by a small number of biologically meaningful parameters such as pigment concentrations, thickness, index of refractions and oblateness of epidermis cells. It can deliver a good model to predict the spectral BDFs of leaves. The results of this approach are shown in Figure 3.3. The LEAFMOD model proposed by

Figure 3.3: Front lit (left) and back lit (right) rendered with the model proposed by Baranoski et al. [12].

Ganapol et al. [36] solves the one-dimensional radiative transfer equation in a slab with homogeneous optical properties and generates an estimate of leaf reflectance and transmittance.

All of these models have in common that they do not take into account the full BSSRDF and do not account for any structures like veins or variations on the leaf surface such as wrinkles and bulges or include the self shadowing of those structures. Including these is imperative to the realistic and convincing rendering of leaves. Also, simulating the radiance transfer through ray tracing on a highly detailed leaf requires an extraordinary amount of calculation time to arrive at a convergent solution. So even for preprocessing, a ray tracing approach is tedious.

Radiative Transfer Models in Real-time Graphics A real-time method to render leaves that uses the LEAFMOD model by Ganapol et al. [36] is proposed by Wang et al. [99]. To generate the used data, as mentioned in Section 3.2.1, a LLS measures both the BRDF and BTDF of the adaxial and abaxial side of a leaf. The results are maps for the diffuse reflectance, specular intensity, roughness and diffuse transmittance of both sides. This data is then fitted to the LEAFMOD model to calculate the thickness variation

CHAPTER 3. LEAF RENDERING

map, albedo map and average of the absorption and scattering coefficient. These maps and values are then used to execute the fitted BDFs in real time.

This is combined with a lighting model that decomposes the lighting into the low-frequency parts of the environment plus the indirect lighting and the high-frequency parts caused by the sun. The low-frequency contributions are modeled with spherical harmonics lighting [92], while the direct sunlight is modeled using an environment map that is calculated by a convolution of the visibility and the sun modeled as a disk. Both parts are preprocessed, saved and evaluated on a per-vertex basis, which makes the method somewhat limited since a high number of vertices is needed to express the high frequency parts of the lighting and requires a large amount of memory. Also, instancing is only possible with the used BSDF parameter maps, which does not allow rendering a large amount of leaves for the display of a full tree for example. Results using this approach can be seen in Figure 3.4. Though

Figure 3.4: Leaves rendered with the method proposed by Wang et al. [99].

this method models the light-leaf interaction on a physical basis, only a one-dimensional transfer is calculated and the detailed structures of a leaf are not incorporated, making the leaves appear too smooth. Also, the question has to be posed why the surface normal is not extracted and used to fit the BDFs instead of using the interpolated normal from the geometry. The most likely problem is that the lighting model used cannot deal with with mapped normals. Since the light-leaf model is tied to the used lighting model, standard methods such as shadow mapping can not be combined with the proposed method, which limits its practicability in full scene or even full plant renderings.

3.2.3 Diffusion-Based Models

For highly scattering media where multi-scattering is a dominant factor, a radiance transfer modeled through path sampling is not completely necessary. The scattering can be treated as a diffusion process as introduced by

3.2. STATE OF THE ART

Stam [94]. Stam solves the diffusion through a multi-grid approach to render the multiple scattering in clouds.

An efficient simulation of subsurface scattering was proposed by Jensen et al. [50], which uses an analytic expression based on the dipole diffusion approximation. It is assumed that the material is homogeneous and semi-infinitely thick. This allows formulating the BSSRDF analytically and has been modified for faster rendering in [49]. It is fast enough to be modified for real-time rendering as shown by Mertens et al. [62] and is used in many publications such as d'Eon et al. [26] to render scattering in different materials.

Donner and Jensen [30] extended this to accurately and efficiently calculate subsurface scattering in multi-layered thin slabs by using a multi-dipole approximation. Since leaves are thin slabs, this extension to the original dipole approximation is applicable to model the light-leaf interaction and is also the basis of the real-time method shown in Section 3.3. Leaves rendered with the multi-dipole approximation can be seen in Figure 3.5. The

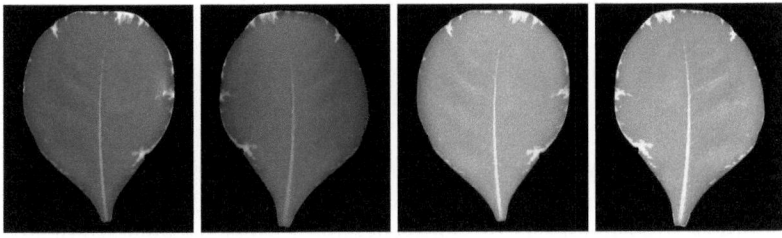

Figure 3.5: Front and back, front lit (left pictures) and back lit (right pictures). (pictures: [30])

model can produce quite realistic results, incorporating effects like different reflectance on the different sides of a leaf. Also, the effect of nearly identical intensities of the transmittance through the different sides is a result of the model rather than originating from the used data, which shows its accuracy.

Franzke et al. [35] showed a simplified single scattering algorithm for leaves based on Jensen et al. [50] by using only the single scattering to model the transfer through a leaf. This reduces the calculation cost significantly but does not include any multi-scattering effects (see Figure 3.6). Besides the dipole diffusion, none of these methods can provide the speed necessary to calculate the scattering in real time.

CHAPTER 3. LEAF RENDERING

Figure 3.6: Plant rendered with single scattering according to Franzke et al. [35].

3.3 A Leaf Model for Real-Time Rendering

Though leaves are very thin, sometimes even below one millimeter, the participating medium is optically thick and thus multiscattering is a dominant part of light scattering in leaves. This leads to a very diffuse translucency because the directionality of any incident light is destroyed and also makes the dipole diffusion approximation a good choice to model scattering in leaves. The dipole approximation can be executed in real-time by undersampling and interpolating the solution. This is a good approach for rendering subsurface scattering of skin on characters for example where the average scattering length is much smaller than the spatial frequencies on the character. The scattering situation inside a leaf is somewhat different because the surface of leaves is not smooth due to the bulges caused by veins or other mesoscopic structures. This does not only have an impact on the reflectance of a leaf, but also has an essential influence on the transmitted light. To achieve a realistic leaf, the scattering needs to be calculated including every detail. Thus, a sparse evaluation followed by an interpolation as done with skin rendering [17, 45], cannot include the defining attributes of leaf translucency. On the other hand, the scattering is very local due to the thinness of leaves and allows reproducing the scattering through a texture based precomputed radiance transfer approach. Based on these insights, a translucency model is presented in the following sections that is tailored for the efficient rendering of leaves.

3.3. A LEAF MODEL FOR REAL-TIME RENDERING

3.3.1 Overview

Before going into details of the real-time rendering of leaves, first, the underlying model and the associated acquisition process is described. Similar to Wang et al. [99], the leaf is modeled as a thin slab of homogeneous material with rough front and back surfaces. The spatially varying reflectance is encoded in an albedo map $\alpha(\vec{x})$, and variations in leaf thickness in a thickness map $d(\vec{x})$. To specify the color of the translucency calculated with the presented model, an average translucency map $\rho_t(\vec{x})$ is used. Finally, a normal map $\vec{n}(\vec{x})$ gives the possibility to accurately simulate high-frequency specular reflections and accurate translucency. All maps exist for both the adaxial and abaxial surface of a leaf.

The light interaction in a leaf is determined by several terms:

$$L = L^{S_d} + L^{S_i} + L^E,$$

i.e. the contribution of direct sunlight, indirect sunlight and environment lighting. The contribution of direct sunlight can be further split into

$$L^{S_d} = L_r + L_t,$$

the reflective and translucent components, where only one is non-zero depending on the dot product between leaf normal and light direction. The shown technique concentrates on the translucency L_t from the direct sunlight illumination since it is the most prominent influence and its directionality causes the translucent part of a leaf to be very dependent on the direction of the sunlight. The indirect or environment illumination L^{S_i}, L^E are approximated by an ambient term in the results. Usually L^{S_i}, L^E already have a low-frequency distribution in their directionality which is then further diffused by the scattering, allowing this approximation by standard techniques. These terms could be calculated following the model of Wang et al. [99] and neglecting the full BSSRDF in those terms.

The data acquisition for the required maps is shown in Section 3.3.2, while the calculation of the reflectance term L_r is covered in Section 3.3.3. The translucency model for L_t, its precomputation and its real-time evaluation is shown in detail in Section 3.3.4.

3.3.2 Data Acquisition

A much more realistic result than creating leaf appearance data algorithmically can be achieved by measuring the data, since nature contains many small imperfections which are automatically captured. In this case, the surface of a leaf is fully reproduced so all structures on its surface, including any

CHAPTER 3. LEAF RENDERING

bending and bulging are incorporated, resulting in a very realistic appearance. The acquisition setup allows generating high-resolution maps (smaller than $1mm$) using a very simple process and off-the-shelf scanning hardware, so even the smallest details, which have an essential impact on both the reflectance and translucence are captured.

The devices used are a 3D scanner operating at an effective resolution of 0.1 mm (Minolta VI-910), a digital camera (Canon EOS 20D) with fixed exposure time, two 1,000 Watt light sources with large box diffusers, and an easy to construct fixing frame for the leaf. The large diffusers are used to approximate hemispherical illumination, which is required for capturing the albedo, removing any directionality in the illumination. The fixing frame guarantees that the leaf remains unchanged during the acquisition process, ensuring the consistency of the acquired data. The leaf is fixed in the frame using wire bridges with small clamps to keep the leaf in a straight but natural position. 3D scanner, camera and diffusers are arranged as shown in Figure 3.7. The leaf is sampled by first taking a 3D scan, then the scanner

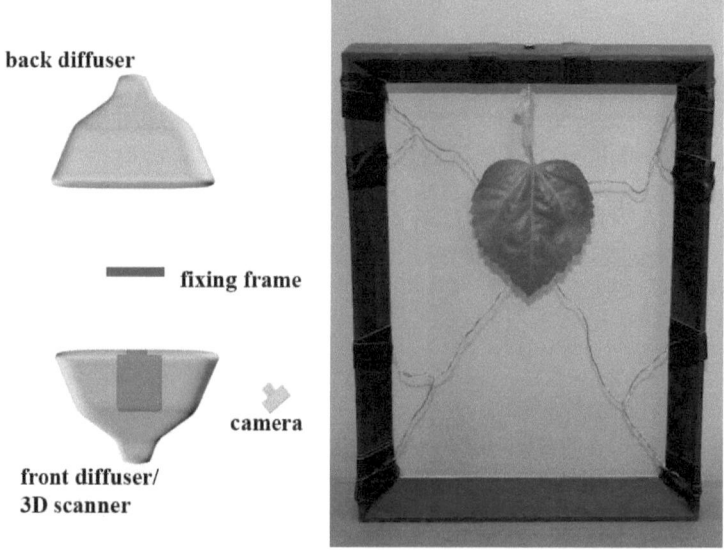

Figure 3.7: Schematics of the acquisition setup and a close up of the fixing frame. For the 3D scan, the 3D scanner replaces the diffuser.

is replaced with a diffuser and the albedo is recorded using the camera. To capture the translucency, the front diffuser is switched off and a picture is taken with the back diffuser on. After carefully turning the fixing frame by

3.3. A LEAF MODEL FOR REAL-TIME RENDERING

180 degrees, the same steps are repeated to process the back side of the leaf.

For postprocessing, standard tools are applied. To process the raw scanned data, Geomagic [2] was used to filter the geometry with a moderate smoothing filter so as not to impact the high-frequency structures, but to remove the high-frequency noise, and to align the scans of the adaxial and abaxial side. Maya was used to create a simplified mesh and to generate highly detailed normal maps [20] and displacement maps for both sides. Further, the thickness map is generated by subtracting the displacement maps, normalized to a user-defined maximum thickness which can also be measured directly on the leaf. The normal maps are not bound to a specific geometry but can be mapped to different geometric levels of detail (see Figure 3.8). Also, low-frequency variations can be generated by using different leaf carrier

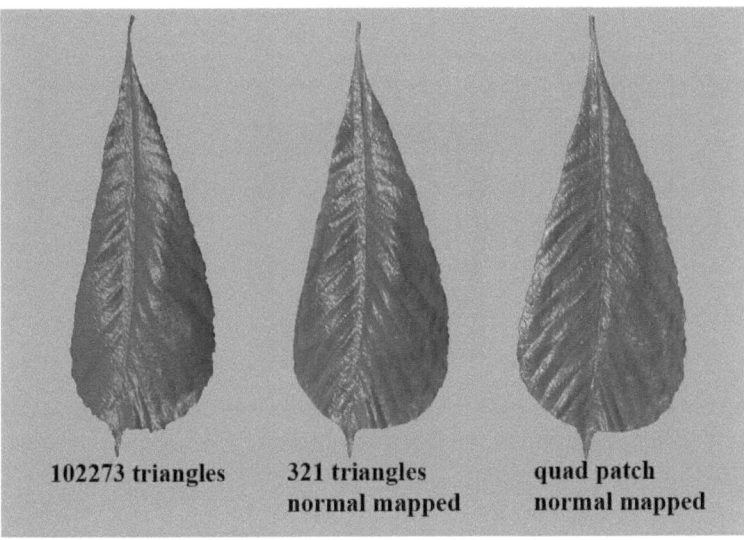

Figure 3.8: The scanned geometry, normal-mapped simplified geometry and the normal map on a quad patch. The highlights have been exaggerated for visualization purposes.

geometries. Depending on the specularity of the measured leaf, the generated albedo maps may need highlight removal using standard image processing techniques. By keeping the exposure fixed, the fact that the albedo on the abaxial side is higher is automatically reproduced in the generated textures. Figure 3.9 shows a complete data set generated using this measurement method. In comparison to the acquisition setup by Wang et al. [99],

CHAPTER 3. LEAF RENDERING

Figure 3.9: A complete data set of a leaf, consisting of albedo (left), translucency (middle) and normal map (right) for both sides and a thickness map (bottom).

the per-pixel BRDF or BTDF data is not captured, requiring a custom-built linear light source device in order to measure both sides. Spatially varying roughness or specular intensity according to measurements cannot be encoded, though hand-produced modulations of BRDF and BSDF parameters are still possible. On the other hand, high-resolution normal maps are created, which causes highlights to be placed more accurately according to the high-frequency structure of the leaf. This is not the case for the method proposed by Wang et al. [99]. This means that without normal maps, any geometric feature needs to be modeled geometrically which is why there are limits to the applicability of their method.

3.3. A LEAF MODEL FOR REAL-TIME RENDERING

3.3.3 Reflectance

The structure of a leaf is mostly perceived in its specular reflectance properties due to direct sunlight illumination (L_r), revealing its high-frequency structures, which are the most prominent features in the illumination and need to be modeled correctly to achieve a realistic leaf rendering. There is a huge variety of leaf BRDFs, ranging from velvet-like due to micro-hairs to highly specular caused by a thick waxy layer. In most cases, the front of a leaf has broad specularity whereas the back of a leaf is diffuse. This is mostly true for broad leaves, but there are also plants which have a highly specular back side, such as *Larrea tridentata*. As with many parts of nature, no general assumptions can be made due to the large variety of plants and their leaves.

Following Bousquet et al. [16] and Wang et al. [99], the Cook-Torrance shading model [22] is used for the front side of the leaf. A simple diffuse model is applied to the back side of the shown leaves. This is not a general limitation, the reflectance attributes of each measured leaf should be examined to match them for a faithful reproduction. Other BRDFs such as Blinn [14] or Schlick [85] are also good choices depending on the physical accuracy required or other factors such as editability or parameter tuning. A BSSRDF approach for reflective subsurface scattering has been considered, but the difference to a standard BRDF model is negligible because the non-directional contribution due to subsurface scattering is included in the albedo map from the acquisition process. This is because in contrast to skin rendering, the subsurface scattering is calculated in a very thin and highly absorbing medium, keeping the range of light diffusion down to a few millimeters at maximum.

As for the parameters of the Cook-Torrance BRDF, the measured and fitted specular coefficients of Bousquet et al. [16] are used. Their measurements define a range of $n = 1.2 - 1.7$ for the effective refractive index and $\sigma = 0.078 - 0.5$ for the roughness, covering highly specular leaves (e.g. *Laurel*) to nearly diffuse specular lobes (e.g. *Hazel*). Figure 3.10 shows leaves with different parameter configuration.

Since high-resolution normal maps were produced, the BRDF is evaluated using the looked-up normals instead of the interpolated geometric normal. The diffuse term is taken from the albedo map. The reflective contribution from direct sunlight, which is modeled as a directional light $L(\omega) = L_D \delta(\vec{\omega} - \vec{\omega}_D)$ with light intensity L_D, light direction $\vec{\omega}_D$, and Dirac function δ, therefore evaluates to:

$$L_r(\vec{x}, \vec{\omega}_o) = L_D \left(\frac{a(\vec{x})}{\pi} + f_s(\vec{n}(\vec{x}), \vec{\omega}_D, \vec{\omega}_o)(\vec{n}(\vec{x}) \cdot \vec{\omega}_D) \right) \quad (3.1)$$

CHAPTER 3. LEAF RENDERING

Figure 3.10: Quad patches shaded with highly specular (top) and almost diffuse (bottom) reflectance, and with a directional light at steep (left) and grazing angle (right).

where $\vec{x}$ is a surface point, $\vec{\omega}_o$ is the outgoing direction and f_s is the specular BRDF. The complete reflective BRDF is thus $f_r = \alpha + f_s$. Note that to arrive at the correct diffuse term, $\alpha(\vec{x})$ would theoretically have to be reduced by the albedo of f_s, however this term is negligible at non-grazing angles.

3.3.4 Translucency

One of the main insights of the shown technique is that while subsurface scattering has only negligible impact on the appearance of the light-facing side of a leaf, it is the dominant factor for the opposite side. Figure 3.11 demonstrates the difference between a simple, yet state-of-the-art translu-

3.3. A LEAF MODEL FOR REAL-TIME RENDERING

cency model based on a diffuse BTDF, and the shown BSSRDF approach. As opposed to the reflective part of the leaf, where high-frequency features

Figure 3.11: Physically based leaf translucency (top) with light at different angles from steep (left) to grazing angles (right) in comparison to the standard diffuse translucency model (bottom).

are conveniently modeled using a normal map, the presented method is the only one which introduces lighting effects due to high-frequency surface variations in the translucent part compared to a simple diffuse shading model using the geometric normal of the leaf. By including these variations, depending on the incident light angle, the leaf appears either smooth at steep angles or shows the influence of the high-frequency details from bulges and veins at grazing light angles (see Figure 3.11).

The main features taken into account by the BSSRDF model are self shadowing of the leaf before the light penetrates into the leaf interior, variations in leaf thickness, and variations of the reflectance properties over the light-facing leaf surface. These effects lead to variations in the amount of light entering the medium and scattering towards a specific point to be shaded on

CHAPTER 3. LEAF RENDERING

the opposite leaf surface. Note that the presented model is local to a leaf, and therefore light variations due to shadows from other leaves or similar only modify the resulting radiance, but do not enter into the subsurface scattering computations. These effects can be handled using standard real-time shadow algorithms. However, the influence of such large-scale structures on subsurface scattering in leaves, which happens on a much smaller scale, is negligible.

To model the BSSRDF light transport through the leaf, the multi-dipole approximation introduced by Donner and Jensen [30] is used. The main concepts of this method are shown in the following section, which are then formulated as an image convolution using the measured data. This model is then used to precompute the exitant radiance as a function of the light direction which is expanded into the Half Life 2 basis.

All calculations are carried out in the tangent space of the simplified geometry, scaled to preserve all physical units. The tangent space can safely be assumed to be locally flat in comparison to the typical length of scattering paths, which is a prerequisite for the used BSSRDF model.

3.3.5 Light Diffusion in Leaves

To model the scattering inside a leaf, it is assumed that the leaf material is homogeneous and characterized by its absorption coefficient σ_a, scattering coefficient σ_s and the mean cosine of the scattering phase function g, which defines if the scattering is isotropic or has a forward or backward trend.

The Bidirectional Scattering Surface Reflectance Distribution Function (BSSRDF) [68] is formally defined by

$$S(\vec{x}_i, \vec{\omega}_i, \vec{x}_o, \vec{\omega}_o) = \frac{dL_o(\vec{x}_o, \vec{\omega}_o)}{d\Phi(\vec{x}_i, \vec{\omega}_i)}, \tag{3.2}$$

where L_o is the outgoing radiance on the non-light facing side and Φ is the incident flux on the light-facing side of the leaf. $\vec{x}_i$ and $\vec{\omega}_i$ are the incident position and direction and $\vec{x}_o$, $\vec{\omega}_o$ are the exitant position and direction. Jensen et al. [50] showed that for a semi-infinite homogeneous slab, the BSSRDF can be approximated by a diffusion dipole, defined by 2 virtual point light sources where a positive light source resides inside the material and a negative light source is above the surface. Both light sources are set so that the boundary condition on the surface are met, which results in the assumption that the material is a semi-infinite slab.

Compared to that, in a thin slab, two boundary conditions have to be taken into account. Light that reaches either the front or the back of the leaf exits the scattering material and never returns. In order to match both

3.3. A LEAF MODEL FOR REAL-TIME RENDERING

the boundary conditions on both surfaces, multiple dipole-pairs are required [30]. The boundary conditions are expressed in terms of the scalar irradiance ϕ, also called *fluence*:

$$\phi(r) - 2AD\frac{\delta\phi(r)}{\delta z} = 0 \quad \text{at } z = 0, z = d \quad (3.3)$$

where $D = \frac{1}{3\sigma'_t}$ with the reduced extinction coefficient $\sigma'_t = \sigma_a + (1-g)\sigma_s$. Expression (3.3) is applied at the front surface at $z = 0$ and the back surface at a depth of $z = d$. The term A represents the change in fluence due to internal reflection at the surface:

$$A = \frac{1+\rho_d}{1-\rho_d}. \quad (3.4)$$

Since leaves have a rough reflective surface, the average diffuse reflection ρ_d of the reflective BRDF f_r is used, which can be evaluated using sampling, instead of a Fresnel term.

In order to match the boundary condition at $z = 0$ given in (3.3), a real positive point light is placed under $\vec{x}_i$ at a depth of one mean free path $l = 1/\sigma'_t$ [72]. By placing a negative virtual light source at $(1 + 4A/3)/\sigma'_t = 2z_b + l$, the net fluence at $-z_b = -2AD$ vanishes and results in a good approximation for the first boundary condition at $z = 0$ [33], creating a dipole configuration. Both the positive and negative light are treated as being inside the participating medium since the negative light source creates the correct boundary conditions for the fluence field. This configuration corresponds to the dipole approximation for subsurface scattering proposed by Jensen et al. [50].

To satisfy the second boundary condition at $z = d$, the existing dipole is mirrored at the extrapolation distance of the second boundary condition at $z = d + z_b$, which in turn needs to be mirrored at z_b again to match the first boundary condition. This iterative process can be continued to infinity where the limit converges to the matching of both boundary conditions.

Following this iteration, the positions $z_{r,j}$ and $z_{v,j}$ of the positive and negative diffusion dipole poles can be expressed with

$$\begin{aligned} z_{r,j} &= 2j(d+2z_b) + l \\ z_{v,j} &= 2j(d+2z_b) - l - 2z_b, \quad j = -n...n. \end{aligned} \quad (3.5)$$

The resulting fluence field is then defined by

$$\phi(r) = \sum_{j=-n}^{n} \frac{\Phi}{4\pi D}\left(\frac{e^{-\sigma_{tr}d_{r,j}}}{d_{r,j}} - \frac{e^{-\sigma_{tr}d_{v,j}}}{d_{v,j}}\right) \quad (3.6)$$

CHAPTER 3. LEAF RENDERING

where $d_{r,i} = |\vec{x}_0 - \vec{x}_{r,j}|$ is the distance from $\vec{x}_0$ to the real light sources, $d_{v,j} = |\vec{x}_0 - \vec{x}_{v,j}|$ the distance to the virtual light sources and $\sigma_{tr} = \sqrt{3\sigma_a \sigma'_t}$ is the effective transport coefficient. Figure 3.12 shows a slice through a leaf along the z axis of the fluence field for one incident radiance point $\vec{x}_i$.

The diffuse transmittance at the non-light facing surface is equal to the gradient of the fluence (3.6), depending on the slab thickness D and the distance $r = |x_o - x_i|$ from the incident point:

$$T(r,d) = -D \frac{\vec{n} \cdot \vec{\nabla}\phi(\vec{x}_0)}{d\Phi(\vec{x}_i, \vec{\omega}_i)} \qquad (3.7)$$

which evaluates to

$$T(r,d) = \sum_{j=-n}^{n} \frac{\alpha'}{4\pi} \left(\frac{(d - z_{r,j})(1 + \sigma_{tr}d_{r,j}e^{-\sigma_{tr}d_{r,j}})}{d_{r,j}^3} \right.$$
$$\left. - \frac{(d - z_{v,j})(1 + \sigma_{tr}d_{v,j}e^{-\sigma_{tr}d_{v,j}})}{d_{v,j}^3} \right), \qquad (3.8)$$

where $\alpha' = \sigma'_s/\sigma'_t$ is the reduced albedo. Figure 3.13 shows the transmittance for a fixed set of physical properties, depending on the thickness d and distance r, revealing an exponential falloff as the thickness increases, and a smooth, Gauss curve-like falloff as the distance increases. This falloff is relatively strong, taking into account the fact that in a very thin slab, most of the light exits the leaf before it can be scattered far away from the entry point. The BSSRDF for translucency is the transmittance within the leaf multiplied by the transmittances at the incident and exiting leaf surfaces:

$$S(\vec{x}_i, \vec{\omega}_i, \vec{x}_o, \vec{\omega}_o) = \rho_t(\vec{x}_i, \vec{\omega}_i) T(r,d) \rho_t(\vec{x}_o, \vec{\omega}_o). \qquad (3.9)$$

Analogue to the entry point, transmittance is used instead of Fresnel terms since the leaf surfaces are rough. To calculate ρ_t, it is assumed that all light which is not reflected is transmitted into the material to be scattered. Therefore, $\rho_t(\vec{x}, \vec{\omega}) = 1 - \rho_d(\vec{x}, \vec{\omega})$, where $\rho_d(\vec{x}, \vec{\omega})$ is the reflective albedo. Note that front and back surfaces have different BRDFs and thus different albedos.

3.3.6 Light diffusion as an image convolution process

In order to achieve a formulation of subsurface scattering that is amendable to process highly detailed leaf measurements, the BSSRDF evaluation is expressed as an image convolution process that operates directly on the maps and values measured by the data acquisition as previously described

3.3. A LEAF MODEL FOR REAL-TIME RENDERING

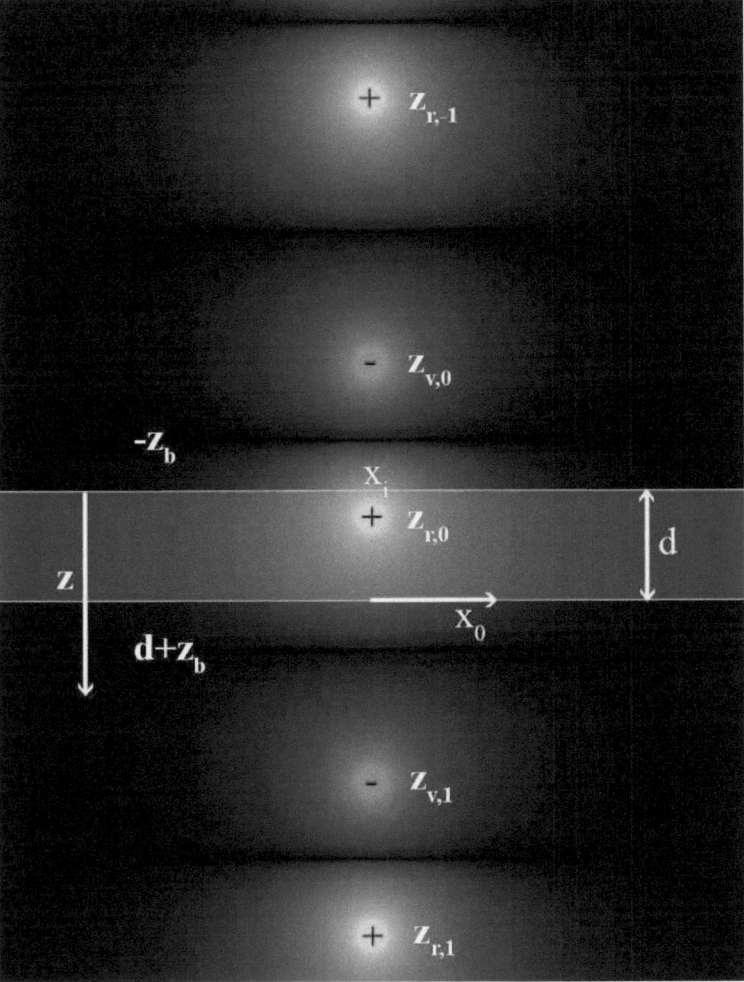

Figure 3.12: Fluence field defined by the multi dipole configuration. Green are positive, red are negative values.

CHAPTER 3. LEAF RENDERING

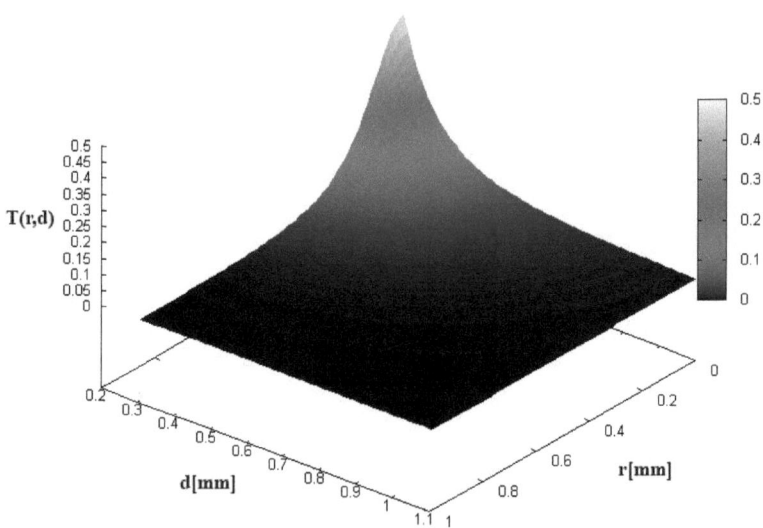

Figure 3.13: Transmittance at different thickness d and distance r for a fixed set of physical properties.

in Section 3.3.2. Reformulating equation (3.2) gives an expression for the translucent radiance:

$$L_t(\vec{x}_o, \vec{\omega}_o) = \int_\Omega \int_A L(\vec{x}_i, \vec{\omega}_i) S(\vec{x}_o, \vec{\omega}_o, \vec{x}_i, \vec{\omega}_i)(\vec{n}(\vec{x}_i) \cdot \vec{\omega}_i) d\vec{x}_i d\vec{\omega}_i \quad (3.10)$$

In this case, one directional light of unit intensity ($L_D = 1$) in direction ω_D is assumed for the precomputation, represented by a Dirac impulse. Later, the result is modulated with the actual light intensity to achieve interactive lighting. Also, self-shadowing from the leaf is taken into account through a visibility term $V(\vec{x}_i, \vec{\omega}_i)$, so that the radiance arriving at $\vec{x}_i$ is

$$L(\vec{x}_i, \vec{\omega}_i) = \delta(\vec{\omega}_i - \vec{\omega}_D) V(\vec{x}_i, \vec{\omega}_i). \quad (3.11)$$

Substituting this and equation (3.9) into (3.10) gives

$$L_t(\vec{x}_o, \vec{\omega}_o, \vec{\omega}_D) = \rho_t(\vec{x}_o, \vec{\omega}_o) \int_A T(r, d) E(\vec{x}_i, \vec{\omega}_D) d\vec{x}_i \quad (3.12)$$

with an irradiance transport function $E(\vec{x}, \vec{\omega})$, which describes the light transport from direction $\vec{\omega}$ to the point $\vec{x}$ just below the surface:

$$E(\vec{x}, \vec{\omega}) = \rho_t(\vec{x}, \vec{\omega}) V(\vec{x}, \vec{\omega})(\vec{n}(\vec{x}) \cdot \vec{\omega}). \quad (3.13)$$

3.3. A LEAF MODEL FOR REAL-TIME RENDERING

Equation (3.12) describes the translucent light transport to $\vec{x}_o$ in a thin slab (leaf) for a given light direction $\vec{\omega}_D$. This equation already has the form of a continuous convolution process of the signal $E(\vec{x}, \vec{\omega})$ with kernel $T(r, d)$ (equation (3.8)).

To take the thickness variations into account, the measured thickness $d(\vec{x}_i)$ is taken as a local approximation of the boundary conditions that lead to the transmittance term. This makes the convolution kernel $T(r, d(\vec{x}_i))$ non-stationary. This local approximation, which is inherent in the multi-dipole model, matches the actual boundary conditions closely in the case of leaves, except for vein sides, which get slightly softer. This is the same approximation that Jensen et al. make, providing only a local approximation of the scattering material. Taking into account arbitrary boundary conditions accurately is still the main limitation of dipole approximations in comparison to a full Monte Carlo simulation [30]. Donner et al. [31] proposed to use a quadrupole configuration to model the subsurface scattering at orthogonal edges and use a weighted interpolation to interpolate arbitrary edges.

Finally, the fact that all spatially variant variables are given in maps with the same resolution is exploited and the continuous convolution is converted into a discrete one by discretizing the area integral. As area element, the constant physical area of a texel A_p in the maps according to the scaled tangent plane is used.

$$L_t(\vec{x}_o, \vec{\omega}_o, \vec{\omega}_D) = \rho_t(\vec{x}_o, \vec{\omega}_o) A_p \sum_{\vec{x}_i} T(r, d(\vec{x}_i)) E(\vec{x}_i, \vec{\omega}_D) \quad (3.14)$$

Now the calculation of L_t can be implemented as an image convolution, using albedo, transmission, thickness and normal maps as input. Please note that although equation (3.14) represents an image convolution, all the variables such as distances are still the physical lengths on the leaf, and apart from discretization, the result is still an exact representation of (3.10). This result is not limited to preprocessing for real-time rendering but can also be used in a physically based ray tracer, integrating over the light direction $\vec{\omega}$ for global illumination.

3.3.7 Real-Time Translucency

The convolution as derived in the previous section, though fitted to the acquired data, is not directly applicable in real time since every leaf rendered would need its own high-resolution convolution. With equation (3.14), the translucency can be calculated for a given light direction $\vec{\omega}_D$ for each pixel $\vec{x}_o$ on the leaf surface.

CHAPTER 3. LEAF RENDERING

By separating this equation, one obtains the *directional* part that only depends on $\vec{\omega}_D$:

$$L_t(\vec{x}_o, \vec{\omega}_o, \vec{\omega}_D) = \rho_t(\vec{x}_o, \vec{\omega}_o) L_t^D(\vec{x}_o, \vec{\omega}_D) \quad (3.15)$$

with

$$L_t^D(\vec{x}_o, \vec{\omega}_D) = A_p \sum_{\vec{x}_i} T(r, d(\vec{x}_i)) E(\vec{x}_i, \vec{\omega}_D) \quad (3.16)$$

For a real-time evaluation, the expensive image convolution can be precomputed, thus requiring new means to efficiently store and evaluate the resulting hemispherical function $L_t^D(\vec{x}_o, \vec{\omega}_D)$ for every pixel. In order to do so, the *Half Life 2 basis* can be used as a directional basis.

Furthermore, the following important simplification for real-time rendering is made: in principle, the function L_t is wavelength dependent, and therefore would have to be evaluated for several spectral bands, which could be done by calculating $L_t(\vec{x}_o, \vec{\omega}_D)$ with a trichromatic convolution, using the measured albedo and transmission coefficients of both sides of the leaf, and color-dependent coefficients. However, the result is far more convincing if one uses the measured average translucency, which contains both $\rho_t(\vec{x}_o)$ and the very complex spectral absorbing behavior and microstructures that appear in a back lit leaf. Also, any form of structure such as dirt are visible in the translucency and included in the rendering. Therefore, the directional part L_t^D is only evaluated for *one dominant wavelength*. In the case of leaves, this is at a wavelength of 510nm because leaves are dominantly green, basically capturing the effects on *luminance* effected by subsurface scattering. If red or colored autumn leaves are to be rendered, this wavelength needs to be corrected for the dominant color. The full chromatic effect in the final exiting transmittance $\rho_t(\vec{x}_o, \vec{\omega}_o)$ is added by substituting this quantity with the captured translucency $\rho_t(\vec{x}_o)$. Here, the view dependence is also dropped due to the fact that it can be considered to be practically diffuse [12].

3.3.8 The Half Life 2 Basis

The Half Life 2 basis (HL2 basis) is a little documented vector basis that was introduced in the Source engine [61] to combine light mapping and normal mapping by expressing the normal map in terms of the HL2 basis and evaluating the light map for the HL2 basis vectors. This works for example for radiosity, which can be interpreted as a linear function of the normal vector. It was also used to achieve normal mapping in combination with spherical harmonics-based precomputed radiance transfer [91], in which case the vectors are interpreted as functions in terms of the dot product.

3.3. A LEAF MODEL FOR REAL-TIME RENDERING

The HL2 basis itself is generated by 3 orthogonal vectors, rotated relative to the tangent coordinate system so that the angle between adjacent vectors projected on the tangent plane is isotropic, and the angle between the tangent plane and each vector is identical (Figure 3.14):

$$\vec{H}_1 = \left(-\tfrac{1}{\sqrt{6}}, -\tfrac{1}{\sqrt{2}}, \tfrac{1}{\sqrt{3}}\right)$$
$$\vec{H}_2 = \left(-\tfrac{1}{\sqrt{6}}, \tfrac{1}{\sqrt{2}}, \tfrac{1}{\sqrt{3}}\right)$$
$$\vec{H}_3 = \left(\sqrt{\tfrac{2}{3}}, 0, \tfrac{1}{\sqrt{3}}\right)$$

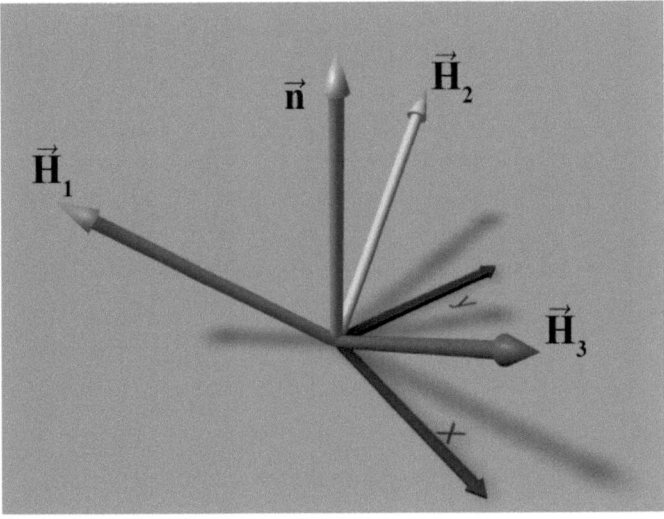

Figure 3.14: The 3 vectors that define the Half Life 2 basis. The colors correspond to their coefficient channel.

These vectors define three cosine basis functions on the hemisphere (see Figure 3.15):

$$\mathcal{H}_i(\vec{\omega}) = \sqrt{\frac{3}{2\pi}} \vec{H}_i \cdot \vec{\omega}. \tag{3.17}$$

The cosine functions do not get clamped, so all basis functions contribute over the whole hemisphere, including negative values where the dot product is negative. This is necessary to achieve the orthogonality of these basis functions which can be verified by their pairwise hemispherical integration:

$$\int_\Omega \mathcal{H}_i(\vec{\omega})\mathcal{H}_j(\vec{\omega})d\vec{\omega} = \delta_{ij}. \tag{3.18}$$

CHAPTER 3. LEAF RENDERING

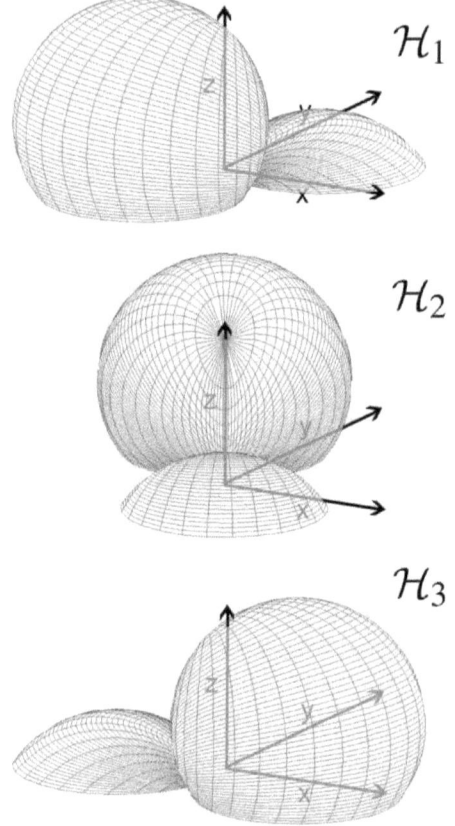

Figure 3.15: The Half Life 2 basis functions. Red are positive and blue are negative values.

3.3. A LEAF MODEL FOR REAL-TIME RENDERING

Therefore, a hemispherical function $f(\vec{\omega})$ can easily be projected into the HL2 basis:

$$f(\vec{\omega}) = \sum_{i=1...3} h_i \mathcal{H}_i(\vec{\omega}) \tag{3.19}$$

using the basis coefficients

$$h_i = \int_\Omega f(\omega)\mathcal{H}_i(\vec{\omega})d\vec{\omega}. \tag{3.20}$$

Even though the hemispherical function represented is always positive, one of the coefficients h_i can be negative in extreme cases.

The advantage of the HL2 basis is that it is very cheap to evaluate the represented function in one given hemispherical direction, which is exactly what is needed for the direct sunlight evaluation. This is in contrast to other hemispherical bases (e.g. spherical harmonics [92] or wavelet bases [57]), requiring the light to be transformed into the used basis, and are therefore preferable only in situations where the illumination itself is also a hemispherical function and not a single direction. Since the basis has only three terms, only low-frequency signals on the hemisphere can be represented, but due to the blurring properties of subsurface scattering, it is sufficient for the shown method.

3.3.9 Projecting Translucency into the HL2 basis

For each position $\vec{x}_o$ on the leaf, the translucency function is projected into the HL2 basis by evaluating equation (3.20) for $L_t^D(\vec{x}_o, \vec{\omega}_D)$. In order to evaluate the hemispherical integral, it is sampled with a uniform distribution of N_L light directions over the hemisphere using Shirley's square to hemisphere mapping [89] to map stratified random points to a hemisphere. $L_t^D(\vec{x}_0, \vec{\omega}_m)$ is extended into the HL2 basis using

$$h_i(\vec{x}_o) = \frac{2\pi}{N_L} \sum_{m=1..N_L} \mathcal{H}_i(\vec{\omega}_m) L_t^D(\vec{x}_o, \vec{\omega}_m) \tag{3.21}$$

where N_L is the total number of lights used.

For each light direction $\vec{\omega}_m$, the image convolution (3.16) is performed using the acquired maps and the convolution kernel $T(r, d(\vec{x}))$. It is not required to convolve every pixel with every pixel. To calculate a maximum size for the kernel, equation (3.8) is evaluated at the thinnest part of the leaf, and the radius where the transmittance falls below a small threshold (10^{-6}) is determined. The result of the projection is a HL2 coefficient map (Figure 3.16).

53

CHAPTER 3. LEAF RENDERING

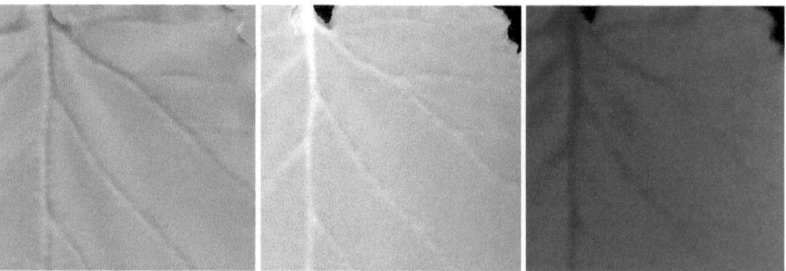

Figure 3.16: The normal map, height map, and the resulting HL2 coefficient map.

It is interesting to note that the special case of perfectly isotropic diffuse translucency $L_t^D(\vec{x}_o, \vec{\omega_D}) = \vec{n} \cdot \vec{\omega_d}$, which corresponds to the diffuse BTDF used in previous work, can be represented exactly using the coefficients $h_i = \sqrt{2\pi}/3$, since $\vec{n} = (0, 0, 1)$ in tangent space and therefore

$$\sum_{1..3} \frac{\sqrt{2\pi}}{3} \mathcal{H}_i(\vec{\omega}_d) = \sum_{1..3} \frac{\sqrt{3}}{3} H_i \vec{\omega}_d = (\sum_{1..3} \frac{\sqrt{3}}{3} H_i) \vec{\omega}_d = \vec{n} \cdot \vec{\omega}_d \qquad (3.22)$$

The coefficients can thus be said to record the deviations of the actual physically based translucency function from this special case.

Precomputing Visibility The image convolution contains an evaluation of the visibility function $V(\vec{x}_i, \vec{\omega}_k)$, which is expensive even for preprocessing since a ray casting to every other pixel would be needed. In order to speed up the projection into the HL2 basis, the visibility term is turned into a lookup by precomputing it in the form of a horizon map per $\vec{x}_i$ [60] to capture the self shadowing of veins and bulges or other structures on the leaf. The horizon circle is divided into 16 slices and the average height for each slice is stored. At convolution time, when evaluating (3.16) in (3.21), the current light direction $\vec{\omega}_m$ is compared to the linearly interpolated horizon to determine if $\vec{\omega}_m$ is above or below the local horizon of $\vec{x}_i$.

Rendering Translucency In order to evaluate the precomputed solution at render time, the light vector $\vec{\omega}_D$ is transformed into tangent space. The HL2 basis coefficients are looked up to evaluate the translucency with

$$L_{t,rec}(\vec{x}_o, \vec{\omega}_D) = L_D \rho_t(\vec{x}_o) \sum_{i=1..3} h_i(\vec{x}_o) \sqrt{\frac{3}{2\pi}} \vec{H}_i \cdot \vec{\omega}_D, \qquad (3.23)$$

resulting in only two texture lookups (ρ_t and h_i are each stored in an RGB texture) and 3 added and weighted dot products.

This computation is extremely simple and memory efficient, and can be integrated into any modern rendering pipeline using pixel shaders. Since only local interactions are considered, the data can be instanced over different leaves while being animated. This allows a large number of leaves to be shaded under dynamic lighting and animation on a per-pixel basis.

3.3.10 Results

To apply the shown technique, the physical parameters need to be set to calculate the subsurface scattering via the image convolution. Measurements from Ma et al. [59] and Woolley et al. [103] give averages, summarized in Table 3.1, together with the parameters of the precomputation. Because L_t^D

Mean cosine	g	0.07
Scattering coeff.	σ_s	10.2 1/mm
Absorption coeff.	σ_a	0.4 1/mm
Refraction index ratio	η	1.33
Multi dipoles	n	3
Number of light directions	N_L	128

Table 3.1: Parameters used for the calculation and precomputation of subsurface scattering.

is evaluated at a wavelength of 510 nm, all parameters are chosen for that wavelength.

In Figure 3.11, the comparison of the presented BSSRDF translucency method with a diffuse BTDF (also applying the acquired maps) using the geometric interpolated normal $\vec{n}_g$ is shown. The diffuse BTDF is calculated with

$$L_t^{BTDF}(\vec{x}_0, \omega_D) = -L_D \rho_t(\vec{x}_0)(\vec{n}_g \cdot \vec{\omega}_D). \quad (3.24)$$

As can be seen, the variations on the surface have an essential impact on the appearance. For example, at steep angles, the structural features are smudged out, whereas at grazing angles the high-frequency structures of leaves are observable. Scattering effects in the leaf due to variations in the light-facing surface, e.g., self shadowing, thickness and reflectance variations, are accurately modeled. In contrast, the standard model appears flat and responds to changes in light direction only through the cosine term. Also, the cases where a leaf is lit on both sides, e.g. when the sun is parallel to the leaf geometry (see Figure 3.17), are rendered fully consistent in both reflectance

CHAPTER 3. LEAF RENDERING

and translucence since the normal map of a directly lit side is taken into account in the translucency part on the other side. A fully rendered tree

Figure 3.17: Leaf on a tree showing fully consistent reflectance and translucency at grazing light directions.

featuring physically based translucency can be seen in Figure 3.18.

Error analysis Since the scattering is precomputed and extended into the Half Life 2 basis, an error occurs due to the frequency limitations. To compare the evaluation of the multi-dipole model with its HL2 basis extension, the relative signal reconstruction error $L_{t,rec}/L_t - 1$ is calculated for all texels in the data set seen in Figure 3.9 for 3 light angles ($\pi/2$, $\pi/4$, $\pi/8$) relative to the orientation of the leaf, measured from the geometric tangent to the normal. The error histogram is shown in Figure 3.19. Figure 3.20 shows a direct comparison at a light angle of $\pi/8$, the worst case of all 3 chosen angles, and corresponding to the blue histogram in Figure 3.19. The average reconstruction error is only 3%, which shows that the Half Life 2 basis is well suited to represent the translucency as a function of direction of incident light. Also, a leaf only transmits about 5-20% [66] of the incident light, an effect accurately modeled with the shown method. This may lead to too dark translucency if leaves are not rendered with physically plausible light intensities and without tone mapping. Fortunately, the HL2 basis coefficients can be scaled without introducing an error to increase the intensity of the translucency.

3.3. A LEAF MODEL FOR REAL-TIME RENDERING

Figure 3.18: A tree featuring physically based translucency.

Implementation and Performance All results were generated on a Pentium4 3.2GHz with an NVIDIA 8800 GTX graphics card running DirectX 10. Starting from the acquired datasets, the precomputation to generate the HL2 coefficient map takes about 20s per image convolution, giving about 45 minutes for a complete leaf dataset. At runtime, the evaluation of the translucency term involves two texture lookups into the translucency and HL2 coefficient map, and a few arithmetic instructions. The cost of this is significantly lower than the rest of the shading model, for example the arithmetic required to evaluate the Cook-Torrance shading model for the light-facing surfaces. The DirectX 10 shader compiler reports approximately 119 instruction slots for the complete shader, of which the translucency part takes about 15 instructions. The technique uses 8 1024x1024 RGB textures: albedo, translucency, normal map and HL2 map, both for front and back sides of the leaf, resulting in 24MB of texture memory for a single leaf dataset which is then instanced over all rendered leaves.

The performance was measured using an interactive application showing a tree with 6,392 leaves rendered as quad patches with normal maps. Each leaf is dynamically shaded. The light-facing leaf sides use the Cook-Torrance shading model, whereas the opposite sides are shaded using the

CHAPTER 3. LEAF RENDERING

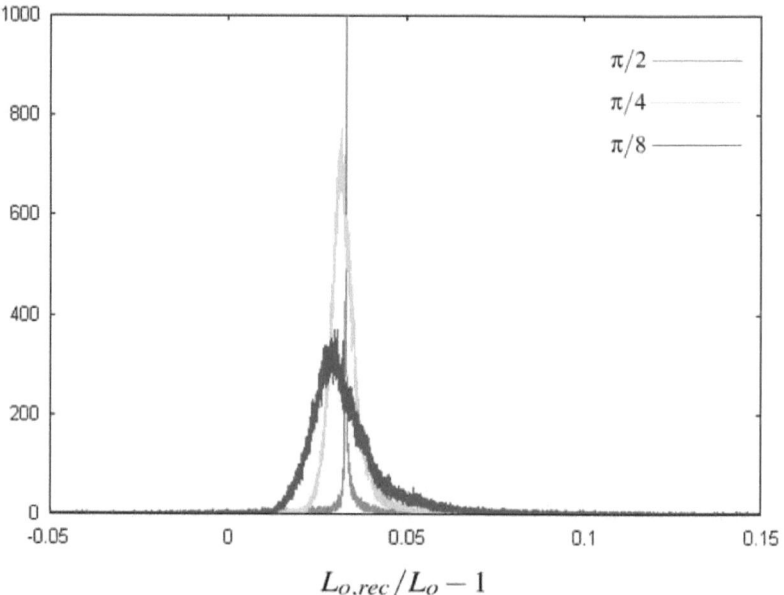

Figure 3.19: Error histogram of the relative signal reconstruction error for 3 light directions.

physically based translucency model. To account for the high dynamic range of the scene, Reinhard's modified tone mapping algorithm [82] is applied together with simple blooming in a post-process. Shadows are generated using a 2048x2048 shadow map which is evaluated with a percentage closer filter (PCF) [81] with 6 Poisson-distributed samples. Indirect lighting is produced with per vertex multi-bounce ambient occlusion, incorporating the translucency of leaves into the indirect lighting calculations. Figure 3.21 shows a comparison of the shown technique to the standard approach. The frame rate for a fly through of the tree varies from 66 frames per second for closeup views where the whole screen is covered with fragments, to 116 fps for more distant views, including all mentioned effects. The datasets for the leaf models, consisting of albedo, translucency, normal, thickness and HL2 basis coefficient maps and an example shader are available at [4].

3.3. A LEAF MODEL FOR REAL-TIME RENDERING

Figure 3.20: Leaf shaded with multi-dipole model L_t (left) and the reconstructed translucency $L_{t,rec}$ (right) at a light angle of $\pi/8$.

3.3.11 Summary

The presented method is the first physically based translucency model for real-time rendering of plant leaves which incorporates the detailed structure of leaves together with the full subsurface scattering. Essential effects like self shadowing, spatially varying reflectance and thickness is accounted for in the simulation. The data can not only significantly improve the translucency, but can also improve the reflectance rendering by using the generated normal maps. Also, the acquisition process does not require any custom built hardware and can deliver highly detailed data. Depending on the 3D Scanner used, a resolution of smaller than 1 mm can be achieved, resulting in a highly realistic rendering of leaves. Additionally, the technique is decoupled from the geometric representation of leaves, making it possible to use the same data set on a quad as well as a high polygon representation as it may be used in levels-of-detail algorithms.

Probably the biggest advantage of the shown technique is that it can be trivially instanced to render a full tree without requiring special treatment. Also, most of the standard techniques such as shadow mapping, light mapping, dynamic lights etc. can be trivially combined with this leaf rendering model without compromising on the quality of the translucency since every detail is correctly incorporated. Also, the integration into existing frameworks is easy since the real-time evaluation is completely shader based and does not require any changes to the rendering besides assigning the shader.

Though no complex lighting such as indirect influences or image-based

CHAPTER 3. LEAF RENDERING

Figure 3.21: A direct comparison of the standard method (left) to the shown method (right) shows improved structure due to normal mapping, and the physically based appearance of translucency in the leaves.

lighting is used, the most important lighting effects are modeled in detail correctly, which is more important than the secondary influences. The shown method can not only be applied to leaves but also to similar structures such as grass blades or blossoms. Also, structured paper, e.g. crumbled paper or watermarks can be modeled accordingly.

For in the true nature of things, if we rightly consider, every green tree is far more glorious than if it were made of gold and silver.
                                Martin Luther

4
Physically Guided Animation of Trees

4.1 Introduction

Plants, especially trees, are an important element of many interactive applications. Almost any outdoor scene features trees or shrubs in some form. Not only realistic rendering, as shown in Chapter 3, is important to recreate a convincing display of vegetation, but also its realistic animation. Due to the small scale structures of vegetation, even in scenes without perceivable wind, there are always some small movements of leaves that are omnipresent in a natural scene, which an observer may not be consciously aware of. Even the most simple animation, as used in Section 2.3.2 for grass for example, improves the perception of any form of vegetation. Though simple forms of animation are easy to achieve, creating visually convincing animation of trees in real time is a difficult problem due to several factors. Trees are geometrically very complex, consisting of thousands of interconnected branches and ten thousands of leaves. These numbers are optimistic, a real adult oak tree can carry around 200 000 leaves, though the given numbers would fit a smaller broad leaf tree. All these geometric elements are connected in a complex dynamic system that is hard to solve and only a few methods have been proposed that provide real-time animation of trees.

4.2 State of the Art

Generally, animating a tree involves a number of components. First, a wind model describes the characteristics of the wind-tree interaction which is coupled with a dynamic system of some form that describes the reaction of branches and leaves to the applied wind force. Usually, the dynamic system incorporates a structural model to define the hierarchical organization.

CHAPTER 4. PHYSICALLY GUIDED ANIMATION OF TREES

Structural elements then define how the results of the dynamic system affect the geometry of the tree, the bending of branches for example. Approaches differ in how these components are implemented, and can be distinguished into two main categories. Those that use heuristic approximations and are fast to compute, and those that try to simulate the physical properties of tree animation more or less accurately. Concerning the structural elements, they can be distinguished into discrete or segment based solutions and approaches that apply structural mechanics models.

4.2.1 Structural Elements

The prevalent structural element model for trees is a skinned or rigid skeletal joint system analogous to rigid or smooth skinning of characters [6, 104, 84, 87, 105, 102]. Many interactive methods simply avoid the problem of bending by not considering any form of deformation [84, 87]. To achieve deformation, a skeletal structure is used to segment single branches in order to model the smooth bending of a branch. With segmented branches, a principal problem occurs since a high number of joints are needed to get convincing results. Additionally, if leaves are represented separately, each leaf requires its own joint. A detailed tree as shown in Figure 4.1 would require about 30,000 joints to achieve a detailed and convincing animation. Also, a joint-based model has the disadvantage that it places a burden on the CPU because the joint matrices for each segment and leaf have to be recalculated every frame which, in the case smooth skinning is applied, have to be accumulated and weighted on a per-vertex basis. On the other hand, an advantage is that the segment joints can be coupled to the dynamic system by applying angular springs for example, which allows the direct integration of the equations of motion. The costly calculations make a joint-based approach prohibitively expensive for high-quality real-time animation of highly detailed trees.

Another approach to model the deformation of branches is to use a structural mechanics model [95, 88, 18]. Structural mechanics is the computation of deformations, deflections, and internal forces or stresses within structures, either for design or for performance evaluation of existing structures. As this is the basis of many engineering sciences, a number of different and highly developed methods exist, though the simpler methods are sufficient to accurately model a branch, as the goal is to achieve a correct appearance and thus strong simplifications can be introduced without compromising the realistic appearance of a deformation. The most used structural mechanics model in context with vegetation is the Euler-Bernoulli model, which will be described in detail in Section 4.4.1, as it is also the basis for the shown approach to calculate the deformation of branches.

4.2. STATE OF THE ART

Figure 4.1: Detailed animated tree.

4.2.2 Animation

To drive the structural model and structural elements, very different methods can be applied, ranging from a full physical simulation to completely heuristic approaches for both the wind model as well as the motion of branches and leaves.

Wind models On the full simulation side, Akagi et al. [6], for example apply a full fluid dynamics simulation, solving the Navier-Stokes equation of an incompressible fluid to model the wind which couples to the joints that are used as structural elements. The equations of motion for the segmented branches are integrated explicitly and feed back to the fluid dynamics simulation to model the full wind-tree interaction. This is of course very expensive and to achieve real-time results, a boundary condition map expressing space distribution of resistances from the tree is used to speed up the calculations. The results of this approach can be seen in Figure 4.2.

To avoid a full fluid dynamics simulation, a stochastic approach from wind engineering can be applied as proposed by Shinya et al. [88] which is also used

CHAPTER 4. PHYSICALLY GUIDED ANIMATION OF TREES

Figure 4.2: Fully simulated tree with fluid dynamics simulated wind. (picture: [6])

by Zhang et al. [104]. Instead of solving the Navier-Stokes equation, wind is modeled as a velocity field with longitudinal, lateral and vertical components. Each fluctuating component of the resulting velocity vectors is modeled by a stationary Gaussian stochastic process. The spatial-temporal properties of the components in the frequency domain are represented by the Cross-Power Spectral Density Matrix to model the coherence of the fluctuations where the FFT (Fast Fourier Transform) delivers the velocity field. Since the fluid simulation is replaced by an FFT, this approach is much faster and still can deliver realistic and physically based wind fields, because turbulent wind can be modeled accurately through a stochastic process. Stam [95] applies a similar model by filtering uncorrelated random velocity vectors for each branch in the frequency domain to achieve a correlation of loads on nearby branches.

Heuristic and hybrid approaches apply much simpler wind models such as a global wind direction or noise functions [87, 93], since a full simulation is not desired.

Dynamic models With joints as structural elements, the integration of the equations of motion can be applied directly [6, 88, 39]. Using even the simplest integration models such as Euler integration, this is prone to be too expensive for a high number of branches since a tree is a highly interconnected system. The integration can be simplified as shown by Sakaguchi et al. [84], where it is assumed that trees are under stationary conditions which allows one not to consider gravity in the calculations. An advantage of a direct

4.2. STATE OF THE ART

integration is that collisions can be taken into account, though resolving the collisions of thousands of branches and leaves and their influence on the dynamic system is impractical on current hardware. Nonetheless, trees and smaller plants that are geometrically simple such as palm trees can be treated that way, allowing full interaction with the environment as shown by the game Crysis [3].

A very successful approach to create vegetation animation is modal analysis. The goal of modal analysis in the context of dynamic models and structural mechanics is to determine the natural mode shapes and frequencies of a structure during free vibration while considering the boundary conditions. As proposed by Stam [95], the simulation is carried out in the frequency domain, reducing computation time by applying spectral methods and avoiding an explicit integration completely. A flexible structure displays certain characteristic shapes when subjected to a force vibrating at one of its modal frequencies. The shape resulting from an arbitrary force can be regarded as a superposition of the modal shapes. The gain of this method is that only a small number of modal shapes corresponding to the smallest modal frequencies contribute to the overall motion of a tree, and only those are used to animate. Figure 4.3 shows a tree that is animated using a modal approach. A drawback of this approach is that since only the most important modal shapes are considered, smaller branches do not perform any independent motion, removing any high-frequency motion from the animation. On the other hand, the modal shapes can be precomputed and and simply superimposed on the GPU, efficiently achieving a physically correct animation without direct intergation. Yung et al. [18] use similar spectral methods to model a large range of natural phenomena. For trees, they consider a simplified, uncoupled dynamic system based on a harmonic oscillator per branch.

A somewhat different approach is taken by Haevre et al.[102]. They apply a technique similar to motion graphs by precalculating a set of motion samples with a dynamic simulation and re-sequence the results at run time. Here, the controllability and directibility and goal-based motion is the focus of this work instead of a fully realistic animation.

Heuristic models Heuristic models do not try to solve the animation problem by means of a simulation, but rather try to emulate the appearance of vegetation movement as efficiently as possible [87, 93] using noise functions to drive the animation.

This usually does not require dedicated structural elements, structural models or elaborate calculations but still can deliver acceptable animation. The simplest approach is to modulate the position of a vertex by a noise

CHAPTER 4. PHYSICALLY GUIDED ANIMATION OF TREES

Figure 4.3: Frames of an animation of a small tree animated with precalculated modal shapes. (picture: [95])

function, disregarding any correlation to the geometric structure. Additional weights, which define the strength and direction of the displacement, can introduce user-defined constraints and a high controllability, which makes this approach very artist friendly and can also emulate the bending of branches on a coarse level [93]. A drawback of a purely vertex-based approach is that it is not possible to calculate correct normals and tangents, essential for advanced shading techniques such as normal mapping or per-pixel lighting. This results from the fact that there is no surface or structure corellation involved and no inverse of the transformation can be calculated. A tree animated using this approach can be seen in Figure 4.4.

Another variation is not to animate on a per-vertex basis, but to drive the joints of a structural model and thus incorporate the structural correlation of a tree. This can be achieved by defining the rotation of branches and leaves with noise functions as proposed by Ota et al. [87] (see Figure 4.5).

To generate the noise functions, different approaches can be applied. The simplest method is to superimpose trigonometric functions and evaluate them in the vertex shader. This has the drawback that the resulting signal is

4.3. HIERARCHICAL VERTEX DISPLACEMENT

Figure 4.4: Frames of an animation of a palm tree using a procedural per vertex animation. (picture: [93])

Figure 4.5: Frames of an animation of a small tree using a procedural approach. (picture: [87])

periodic and a high number of functions need to be superimposed to arrive at a sufficiently complex result. A similar but more efficient approach is taken by Sousa [93], who uses triangle waves which are smoothed out by a cubic interpolation. A more sophisticated generation method is used by Ota et al. [87]. The signal is defined in the frequency domain and transformed into the time domain, allowing to set the power spectrum of the signal. Since the frequency distribution is the defining attribute of the movements of vegetation, this is a very successful method to generate noise functions intended for vegetation animation.

The approach shown in the following sections is a combination of a heuristic and simulation approach, as no simulation is performed at runtime, but the parameters and used data are physically guided to get as close to a simulation as possible without spending the resources a full simulation needs.

4.3 Hierarchical Vertex Displacement

The key element for real-time performance is to *localize* all computations in a vertex shader, leading to so-called vertex displacement. This is often used to animate simple vegetation represented as billboards (e.g., grass) or billboard clouds (e.g. simple tree models). For full geometry models, this is

CHAPTER 4. PHYSICALLY GUIDED ANIMATION OF TREES

not straight-forward.

The general approach is to expose all relevant information of the tree structure, i.e. the hierarchy of the structural model, to every vertex. Thus, the hierarchical deformations of all parent branches can be explicitly performed inside the vertex shader and no information needs to be propagated at runtime. This can be achieved by assigning each vertex an index into a texture that holds all necessary information. This means that every vertex within a branch has the same index. Additionally, as sub-branches can emanate at any position on its parent branch, the relations of each vertex to all parent hierarchy levels are required. To have this data exposed to each vertex, the normalized local coordinate $x \in [0..1]$ of the vertex is precalculated as a scalar per vertex, where x is along the principal axis of a branch. Also, the x-values at parent-branch connections are calculated and propagated down the branch hierarchy (see Figure 4.6). These values are stored

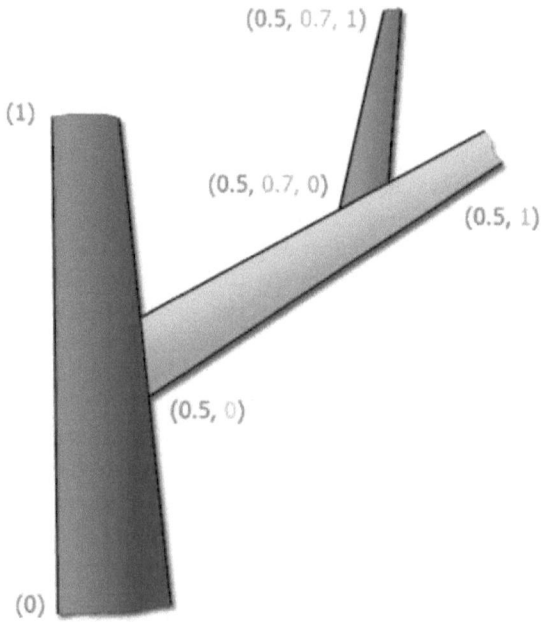

Figure 4.6: $\vec{w}$ distribution of branches in a tree.

with each vertex in addition to its own x-value. The shown trees have 4 hierarchy levels, so each vertex has a vector $\vec{w}$ of 4 values associated in addition to the branch index. A problem that occurs with hierarchical vertex displacement is that the used deformation model that defines the structural elements needs to be able to correctly transform the local coordinate axes between hierarchy levels, so tangent and normal transformations need to be available in order to transform local coordinate systems as well.

4.4 Beam Model

The model used for describing the geometry and physics of a branch as a beam determines how realistic branches swaying in the wind appear to the viewer. A common approximation for realistic animation systems is to model the beam as an elastic cylinder (uniform beam) using structural mechanics, and describe the deformation due to a uniform traversal force using a polynomial deflection function depending on the basic physical properties of the beam. However, uniform beams are not a good approximation for tree branches, as branches are not uniform beams but thin out (taper) at their free end, which has an essential impact on the bending behavior. This taper leads to the effect that tips are much more flexible than thicker parts, which is not accounted for in a uniform beam model. Also, the length needs to be taken care of to achieve a convincing deformation.

To incorporate all those effects, the following sections describe a beam model that takes all basic physical properties of a branch into account. The model still has a closed form solution, allowing for the required tangent and normal transformations, and does not break the restrictions of hierarchical displacement (Section 4.3).

4.4.1 Euler-Bernoulli Beam Model

The Euler-Bernoulli Beam model is a structural mechanics model for long and thin beams with a length to thickness ratio of 15:1 and above, and is therefore suitable for trunks and branches [97]. It is a simplification of the linear theory of elasticity and provides the ability to calculate the deflection characteristics of general beams.

A branch is treated as a linearly tapered circular beam as seen in Figure 4.7, defined by its length L and the radii s_1, s_2 at the root and free end, thus incorporating the essential physical properties of a branch or trunk. The deflection of a branch is described by the Euler-Bernoulli differential equation

$$\frac{\partial^2}{\partial x^2}(EI(x)\frac{\partial^2 u(x)}{\partial x^2}) = F \qquad (4.1)$$

CHAPTER 4. PHYSICALLY GUIDED ANIMATION OF TREES

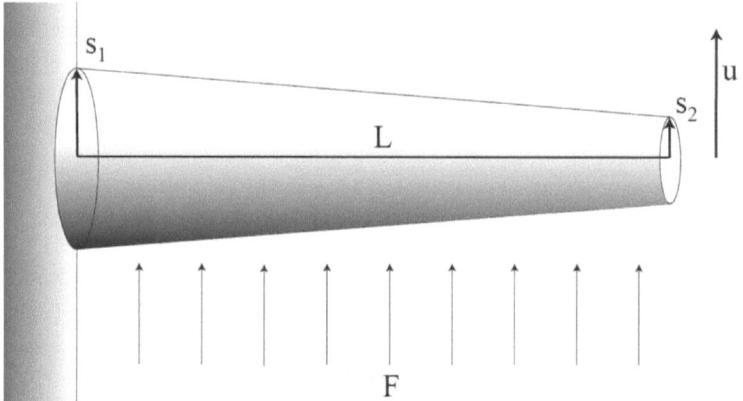

Figure 4.7: Beam model used to calculate the deflection of branches.

where $u(x)$ is the (unknown) deflection of the beam according to the constant transversal force F. I is the area moment of inertia, not to be confused with the mass moment of inertia, and E is the elastic modulus, which is assumed to be constant.

As each branch is fixed at its root, the boundary conditions are

$$u|_{x=0} = 0 \qquad \frac{\partial u}{\partial x}|_{x=0} = 0. \qquad (4.2)$$

The boundary conditions at the free end are

$$\frac{\partial^2 u}{\partial x^2}|_{x=L} = 0 \qquad \frac{\partial^3 u}{\partial x^3}|_{x=L} = 0. \qquad (4.3)$$

To simplify the solution and to fit it to the hierarchical vertex displacement data in Section 4.3, the model is normalized to unit length by scaling the radii by L, and introduce the taper ratio α of the two radii

$$r_{1,2} = \frac{s_{1,2}}{L} \qquad \alpha = \frac{r_2}{r_1} \qquad (4.4)$$

and a rescaled elasticity modulus $E' = EL$. The area moment of inertia for a circular area corresponding to the beam axis is

$$I = \frac{\pi r^4}{4} \qquad (4.5)$$

with the radius varying linearly over the length of the beam. Here the importance of the taper of a branch becomes evident as the area moment is a

4.4. BEAM MODEL

quartic function of the radius, thus significantly affecting the resulting deflection as the radius varies. The area moment of inertia along the beam results in

$$I(x) = \frac{\pi r_1^4((\alpha - 1)x + 1)^4}{4}. \quad (4.6)$$

Under the given boundary conditions (4.2) (4.3) and varying $I(x)$ (4.6), the Euler-Bernoulli Equation (4.1) has an analytical yet not trivial solution

$$\begin{aligned} u(x) &= \frac{E'F}{r_1^4}(x(\alpha - 1)(6 + x(\alpha - 1)(2x(\alpha - 1)(3 + (\alpha - 3)\alpha) \\ &+ 3(4 + (\alpha - 2)\alpha))) - 6(1 + x(\alpha - 1))^2 \log(1 + x(\alpha - 1))) \\ &\cdot \left(3\pi(1 + x(\alpha - 1))^2(\alpha - 1)^4\right)^{-1}. \end{aligned} \quad (4.7)$$

It is interesting to note that the force F affects the solution linearly, which means that the amplitude of the deflection $u(x)$ is proportional to F, while the root radius influences the deflection with r_1^{-4}. Figure 4.8 shows the deflection for different taper ratios normed to $E'F/r_1^4 = 1$. As can be seen,

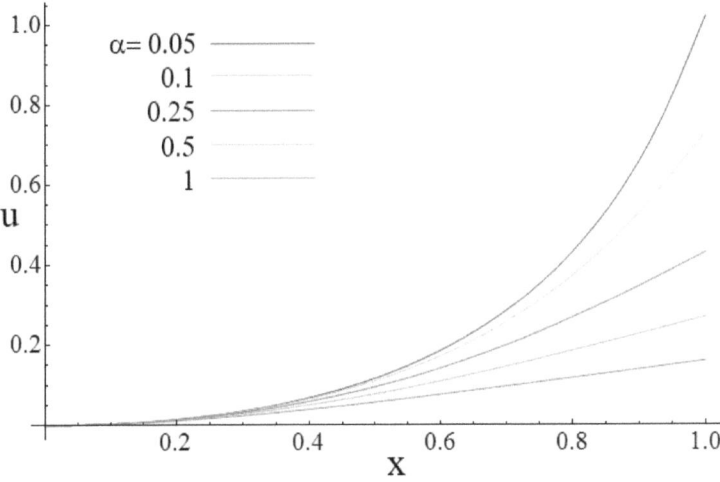

Figure 4.8: Deflection for different taper ratios. With decreasing taper ratio, the beam deflection increases due to the thinning of the branch.

the taper of a branch has a very strong influence on both the deflection amplitude and the form of the deflection and can not be neglected in a realistic branch model. A beam with no taper ($\alpha = 1$) as commonly used

CHAPTER 4. PHYSICALLY GUIDED ANIMATION OF TREES

α	c_2	c_4	Δx_{max}
0.05	0.221875	0.754029	0.0469
0.1	0.3326	0.398924	0.0024
0.2	0.374571	0.129428	0.0081
0.3	0.364816	0.024577	0.006

Table 4.1: Coefficients for equation (4.8) of different values of the taper ratio α.

(e.g. [88]) deflects in a way that the free end is nearly linear, compared to a very curved and stronger deflection along the beam at small taper ratios.

It is inefficient to execute equation (4.7) in a vertex shader, therefore, in order to speed up the calculation of $u(x)$, a linear least square fit to the polynomial

$$u(x) = c_2 x^2 + c_4 x^4 \qquad (4.8)$$

is performed, depending on the taper ratio of each branch. Table 4.1 shows coefficients for some normed taper ratios, along with the maximum absolute error Δx_{max} of this approximation. For taper ratios above 0.1, the fit is virtually exact. Through the absolute fit, α, E' and r_1 are represented by the coefficients c_2 and c_4.

4.4.2 Length Correction

The Euler Bernoulli beam model works well for small deflections, but strong deflections (amplitude $> L/4$) show noticeable stretching since the deflection is only applied in the transverse direction. Unfortunately, the exact incorporation of the length requires the solution of an elliptical integral [13] which can not be formulated explicitly. In order to length correct a deflected

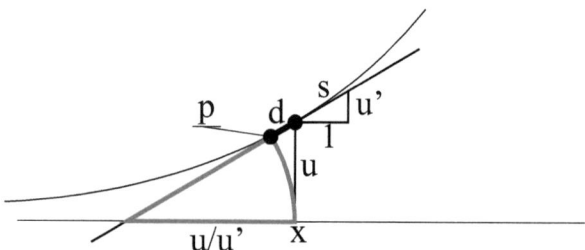

Figure 4.9: Geometry of the length correction. (parameter x omitted for clarity).

4.4. BEAM MODEL

branch, the stretch introduced by the shear of (4.8) is corrected by moving the deflected vertex along its tangent, effectively converting the shear into a rotation. Using the stretch factor of the shear (which is also the length of the tangent vector), $s(x) = \sqrt{1 + u'^2(x)}$, the local length difference $d(x)$ of the original and deflected beam is

$$d(x) = \frac{u(x)}{u'(x)}(s(x) - 1). \tag{4.9}$$

Starting from an original point on a branch $\vec{p}_o = (x, y)^T$, the uncorrected point would be $\vec{p}_u = (x, y + u(x))^T$. The final deflected point $\vec{p}$ can be found by moving the originally deflected point $\vec{p}_u$ along the tangent direction to unstretch the beam (see Figure 4.9):

$$\begin{aligned} \vec{p}_x &= x - \frac{d(x)}{s(x)} \\ \vec{p}_y &= y + u(x) - \frac{u'(x)d(x)}{s(x)} = y + \frac{u(x)}{s(x)} \end{aligned} \tag{4.10}$$

with $x \in [0..1]$. Thus, the original point is deflected using the offset vector $o(x)$:

$$\vec{p} = \vec{p}_o + \vec{o}(x), \qquad \vec{o}(x) = \frac{1}{s(x)}\begin{pmatrix} -d(x) \\ u(x) \end{pmatrix} \tag{4.11}$$

Figure 4.10 compares a strong deflection to its corrected deformation. Though

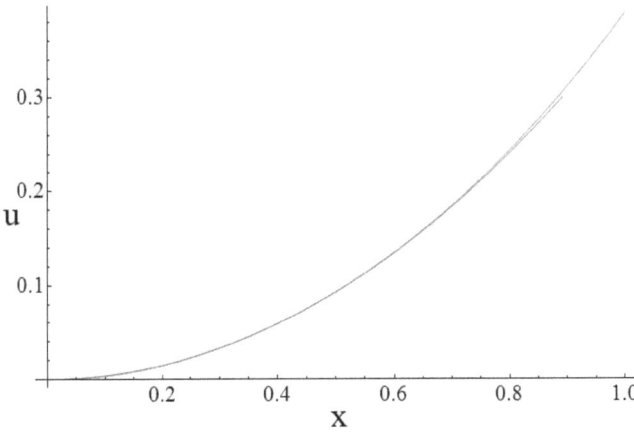

Figure 4.10: Strongly deflected and length corrected beam.

the correction is linear, the result is very close to the fully correct solution due to the fact that the deflection is essentially a quadratic function.

CHAPTER 4. PHYSICALLY GUIDED ANIMATION OF TREES

4.4.3 Branch Deformation

The previous section derived a 2D deflection operator for a unit-length beam. In order to apply the deflection and length correction to the vertices of an arbitrary branch, the deflection needs to be expressed in the local coordinate system of the branch and un-normalized to the original branch length L. It is assumed that each vertex is given in the local coordinate frame $(\vec{t}, \vec{r}, \vec{s})$ of the branch, where $\vec{t}$ goes along the axis of the beam (see Figure 4.11). Let

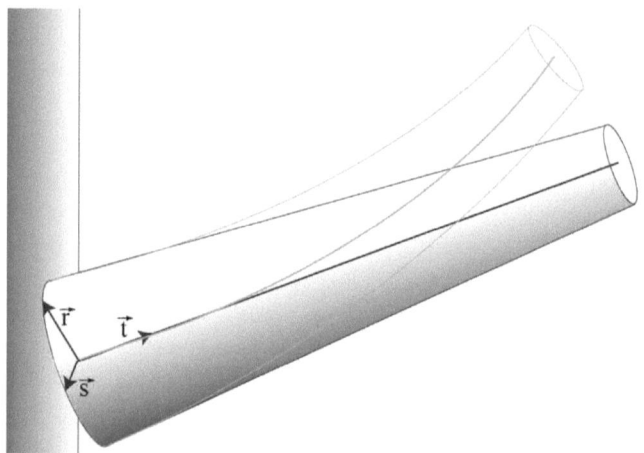

Figure 4.11: Local coordinates for a branch.

$\bar{x}$ be the coordinate along $\vec{t}$, then $x = \bar{x}/L, x \in [0..1]$, and the un-normalized deflection function $\bar{u}(\bar{x}) = u(x)$. By the chain rule, $\partial \bar{u}/\partial \bar{x} = 1/L \partial u/\partial x$.

To take care of the amplitude of the deformation, the amplitude $\vec{A}$, which is proportional to the net force acting on the branch, is projected onto $\vec{r}$ and $\vec{s}$, and the deflection is multiplied with the corresponding amplitudes A_r and A_s to arrive at deflection curves in the two directions, using the normalized coordinate x:

$$u_{r,s}(x) = A_{r,s} u(x), \qquad u'_{r,s}(x) = A_{r,s} \frac{u'(x)}{L} \qquad (4.12)$$

$A_{r,s}$ does not directly set the strength of the deflection since taper ratios and radii vary from branch to branch. The resulting 3D position is thus

$$\vec{p} = \vec{p}_o + \vec{o}(x), \quad \vec{o}(x) = \begin{pmatrix} -d_r(x)/s_r(x) - d_s(x)/s_s(x) \\ u_r(x)/s_r(x) \\ u_s(x)/s_s(x). \end{pmatrix} \qquad (4.13)$$

4.4. BEAM MODEL

To transform tangents and normals, the Jacobian J_p of this transformation would have to be calculated. However, the length-corrected deformation leads to several complex higher order terms which are difficult and expensive to evaluate in real time. Therefore, the Jacobian J_{p_u} of the non-length corrected deflection evaluated at the length corrected position, is used:

$$J_{p_u} = \begin{pmatrix} 1 & 0 & 0 \\ u'_r(x - d_r(x)/s_r(x)) & 1 & 0 \\ u'_s(x - d_s(x)/s_r(x)) & 0 & 1 \end{pmatrix} \quad (4.14)$$

to find the deflected (un-normalized) tangents as $\vec{t} = J_{p_u}\vec{t}_o$, and the deflected (unnormalized) normals as $\vec{n} = J_{p_u}^{-T}\vec{n}_o$, where $\vec{t}_o, \vec{n}_o$ are the tangent and normal vectors of a vertex projected into the local frame of a branch. The error introduced is minimal (a maximum 2.4 degrees for the tip of the beam) since the derivatives of the deflected curve and the length corrected curve are virtually the same for the same x (see Figure 4.10).

This deformation is then applied hierarchically, including all sub-branches in order to have them follow the movements of their parent branches correctly as seen in Figure 4.12.

Figure 4.12: Branch including sub-branches in the undeformed (left) and a deformed (right) state. The sub-branches follow the deformation correctly.

4.5 Synthesizing Branch Motion

A tree interacting with wind is a highly complex dynamic system that is difficult to solve through numerical simulation while upholding the restrictions of hierarchical vertex displacement, not allowing access to previous states. To simplify the dynamic system, it is treated as an uncoupled system of harmonic oscillators per branch. The basis of this simplification is that an observer cannot judge the correctness of the response function of the highly complex dynamical system because the wind itself is not visible. Thus, the characteristics of the animation are mainly determined by the frequencies and amplitudes of branches and not by their exact functional values.

To avoid explicit integration of the equations of motion, *spectral methods* similar to [18] are used to synthesize branch motion to drive the branch deformation. The principal idea is to generate noise functions that obey the same frequency distributions as empirically observed data or results of a full simulation.

In this section, an optimized method is shown to synthesize noise functions that allow fully aperiodic motion for a whole tree using only a small number of noise textures, making the method well suited for real-time applications. Also, a simple wind model is additionally applied in order to define a wind direction leaves and branches react to.

4.5.1 Turbulent Wind and Motion

Trees cause the wind acting upon them to become much more turbulent than free flowing wind. The turbulence in the wind field is dominant over the directional contribution, making it hard to tell the wind direction from tree motion in low or medium wind. As there is no dominant direction, it is possible to model wind velocity using its power spectrum. A common model has been created from empirical data [90]:

$$P_w(f) \propto \frac{v_m}{(1 + f/v_m)^{\frac{5}{3}}} \qquad (4.15)$$

where v_m is the mean velocity of the wind.

The overall motion of a branch can be approximated using the physical model of a damped harmonic oscillator, incorporating the dynamic properties of a branch such as its resonance frequency f_h, mass m, and damping γ_h caused for example by the leaves' resistance to wind and internal damping. While coupling due to the branch hierarchy can be incorporated at higher processing and memory cost [95], a reasonable assumption is that each branch oscillates about its root independently [18]. This is mainly because due to the

4.5. SYNTHESIZING BRANCH MOTION

typically different branch lengths at different hierarchy levels, the resonance frequencies are far apart and the sub-branches are dragging along at the parents' frequency.

The amplitude spectrum of the *stationary solution* of a harmonic oscillator with its resonance frequency f_h and damping γ_h, driven by an external force (4.15) is given by:

$$V_h(f) = \frac{V_w(f)}{2\pi m(2\pi(f_h^2 - f^2)^2 + (2\pi f \gamma_h)^2)^{\frac{1}{2}}} \quad (4.16)$$

where $V_w(f)$ is the force spectrum of wind. A light form of coupling between branches is introduced by calculating the mass m of each oscillator from the branch itself and all its sub-branches, with ρ_w being the density of wood:

$$m = \rho_w \sum_i \frac{\pi L_i}{3}(s_{i,1}^2 + s_{i,1}s_{i,2} + s_{i,2}^2). \quad (4.17)$$

Equation (4.17) is the sum over the volumes of the truncated cones of the branch itself and all sub-branches.

4.5.2 Stochastic Motion Synthesis

To synthesize motion in the time domain, the noise itself is generated in the frequency domain where the wind and oscillator response functions define the power spectrum. The back transform gives the signal in the time domain, hence the name "spectral method". More specifically, a "noisy" wind force spectrum is generated by modulating a random Gaussian field $G(f)$ by the square root of the power spectrum of wind:

$$P'_w(f) = G(f)\sqrt{P_w(f)}. \quad (4.18)$$

Similar to [18], wind force is assumed to be proportional to wind velocity:

$$V_w(f) \propto P'_w(f). \quad (4.19)$$

Plugging this into (4.16) and taking the inverse Fourier transform of $V_h(f)$ gives the motion texture in the time domain. Phase shifts do not have to be considered since the phases of the Gaussian field as well as the resulting velocity spectrum are both uniformly distributed. Though other noise generation approaches such as Perlin noise [75] can also be used for a non-physical approach, the incorporation of effects such as resonance frequencies and a physically correct wind spectrum provide the means to get much closer to the result of a physical simulation than completely heuristic approaches.

4.5.3 2D Motion Textures

The process described so far gives 1D noise functions in the time domain. But realistic trees have thousands of branches, requiring a massive number of different noise functions, all of which should be aperiodic.

To avoid the individual generation and evaluation, the presented motion synthesis method uses *2D motion textures* instead of 1D functions. The velocity spectrum can be written as $V_h(f) = G(f)H(f)$, with $H(f)$ representing the combined spectral response function of the harmonic oscillator and wind. Instead of a 1D generation, a 2D random Gaussian field $G(x, y)$ is initiated and a 2D velocity spectrum $V_h(x, y) = G(x, y)V_h(\sqrt{x^2 + y^2})$ is calculated. The corresponding 2D motion texture is the inverse Fourier transform of $V_h(x, y)$.

Trajectories. For the evaluation of a 2D motion texture, a linear trajectory of a texture sample point can be defined, sampling the 2D-periodic (due to the Fourier transform) motion texture with texture repeat for values outside the unit square. Since the spectrum is radially symmetric in the frequency domain, each such trajectory creates a 1D signal with a spectrum of $V_h(f)$. Furthermore, such trajectories are *aperiodic* as long as the trajectory does not close on itself. To avoid this case, the irrationality of the vector component ratio m_x/m_y is tested and rejected if the ratio of the vector components is very close to a rational value with a small nominator and denominator. Figure 4.13 shows an example trajectory through a motion texture and its result.

Usage for branches. The 2D motion textures are exploited in two different ways. First, all trajectories through the texture are aperiodic, thus the tree animation will not show any periodic motion artifacts. Second, the memory requirements for motion generation is strongly reduced. Instead of generating separate motion functions for each branch, just one 2D motion texture for each hierarchy level is used and each individual trajectory, defined by unique random vectors, delivers a one dimensional signal.

The physical properties that enter the computation of a motion texture are averaged from all branches at the corresponding hierarchy level. While this approach ignores differences in some physical attributes of branches at the same hierarchy level, this is a valid approximation since these branches have roughly the same properties and attributes, such as number of subbranches and leaves attached.

4.5. SYNTHESIZING BRANCH MOTION

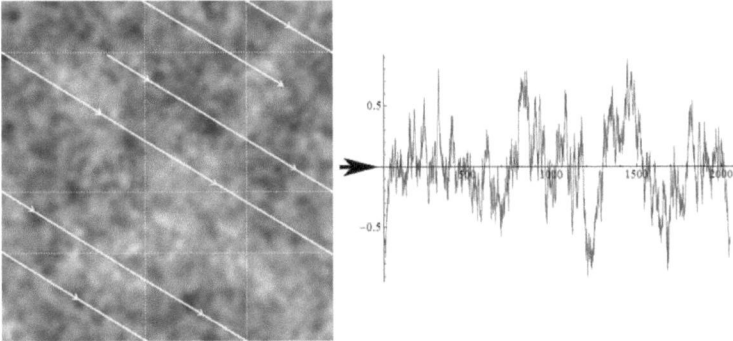

Figure 4.13: Example wrapped trajectory through the motion texture (left) which results in a aperiodic signal with a defined spectrum (right).

Branch frequencies. As the signal is evaluated from a trajectory in the time domain, there is one way to reintroduce variation within a hierarchy level. Instead of following the trajectory with the exact speed determined by the f_h which was used to create the texture, f_h is varied individually by varying the length of the motion vector $\vec{m}$ for each branch. This effectively scales the spectrum of $V_h(f)$ in the time domain. In order to determine an appropriate f_h for each branch, empirical data from [19] is used, which incorporates complex effects such as the dragging forces and internal damping of a branch, giving

$$f_h = 2.55 L^{-0.59}. \qquad (4.20)$$

Thus, each branch has its own resonant frequency according to its length. Since branches in one hierarchy level have roughly similar lengths, the rescaling is small and the difference to a motion texture calculated using f_h in the first place is imperceptible. This empirical result is based on broad leaf trees and needs to be modified for leafless branches or fir tree branches which behave differently. According to [19], leafless branches have approximately 2.5 times the frequency calculated by equation (4.20).

Signal smoothing. The inverse Fourier Transform generates textures where the highest frequency is 2 texels per cycle. A good reconstruction of such a signal would require an appropriate reconstruction filter (e.g., sinc). However, graphics hardware provides only linear filtering, which would lead to unpleasant motion artifacts. Therefore, the motion texture is *prefiltered*.

CHAPTER 4. PHYSICALLY GUIDED ANIMATION OF TREES

Since the noise is generated in the frequency domain, this can be easily done by applying a box filter. In practice, the function is generated with the desired frequency range, and is then extended by a factor of 4, padding the additional frequencies with 0. The resulting motion texture has a highest frequency of 8 texels per cycle, giving a smooth result after linear interpolation. Since it is the frequency range around the resonance frequency which needs to be represented best, $f_{max} = 2f_h$ is set as the maximum frequency represented in the box region. The lowest representable frequency is thus $f_{min} = f_{max}/(8res)$, where res is the texture resolution. Though eight samples per cycle are not enough to fully reproduce a smooth signal, the highest represented frequency amplitudes are very small compared to the dominant frequency (either the lowest frequency or the resonance frequency) as seen in Figure 4.14.

Damping. Damping is one of the critical parameters in determining branch motion. Figure 4.14 shows the spectra and parts of the resulting texture in the under-damped (low γ_f) and overdamped (high γ_f) case. In the former case, the resonance frequency is dominant and will show up in the time domain accordingly, whereas the latter case hides the resonance frequency. The overdamped case has a spectrum very close to a $1/f^\beta$ with $\beta \approx 2$, explaining why $1/f^\beta$ noise can be used to approximate the motion in some cases (as in [87]). However, it is important to take branch physics into account since simply using $1/f^\beta$ noise cannot account for the resonance of branches due to the turbulent wind, which is essential in most cases.

In practice, it is hard to estimate the damping coefficient γ_h of branches, as it depends on parameters such as the leaf mass, leaf distribution as well as redistribution during movements and the viscoelastic damping of wood. All the mentioned influences are strongly non-linear and very complex in their impact on the behavior of a branch. Furthermore, trees targeted at real-time graphics are modeled after their appearance and not according to the correct dynamics and geometry of a tree, which leads to unsatisfactory results if γ_h is derived from the given geometry. A comparison of empirical measurements [65] suggests values of γ_h in the slightly underdamped region, whereas large branches with a large number of sub-branches and leaves are close to the critically damped case. The reason for this is that a tree needs to be stiff enough to uphold itself and to be flexible enough to withstand strong winds. A configuration that is close to the overdamped case avoids any resonance catastrophe while the energy taken from the wind can quickly dissipate into the deformation.

4.5. SYNTHESIZING BRANCH MOTION

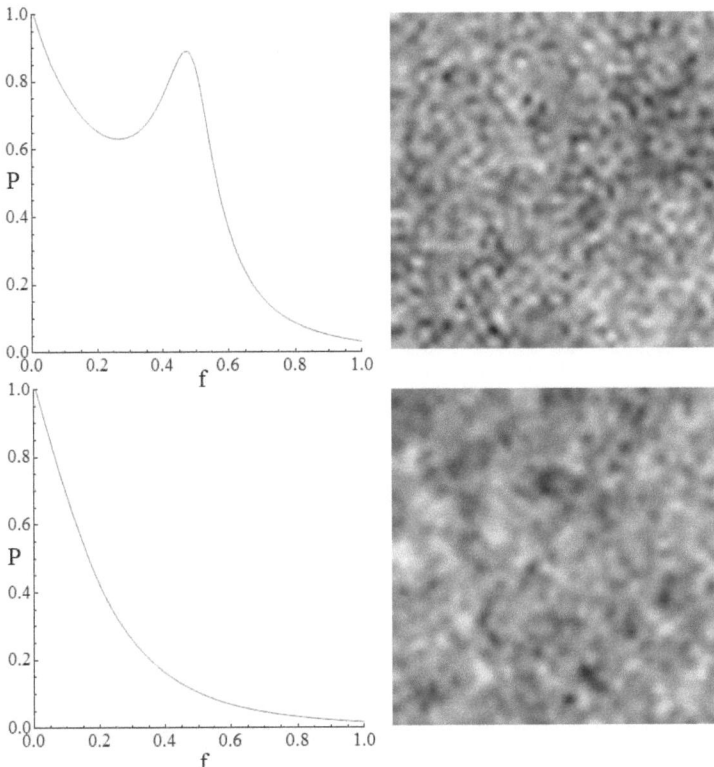

Figure 4.14: Spectra and parts of the resulting textures for the damped (top) and the overdamped case (bottom).

4.5.4 Wind Direction

As already mentioned, the wind direction is not essential for slight to medium winds, which are governed by turbulence. Stronger winds, however, will cause large branches that are orthogonal to the wind direction $\vec{W}$ to receive a directional force that causes strong bending in the wind direction. To model that behavior, for each branch the turbulent wind amplitude is offset by the force of the strong wind component according to the orientation of the branch, given by its local frame:

$$A'_r = A_r + (\vec{r} \cdot \vec{W}) \quad (4.21)$$
$$A'_s = A_s + (\vec{s} \cdot \vec{W}). \quad (4.22)$$

CHAPTER 4. PHYSICALLY GUIDED ANIMATION OF TREES

Superimposed with the spectrally based motion generation, the resulting movement of the branches generally follows the wind direction. Since the local coordinate systems of every individual branch are evaluated, the behavior is correct through all hierarchy levels. To introduce variation, the wind strength (length of $\vec{W}$) can be modulated with a very low frequency noise to emulate long time variations.

4.6 Applying Beam Deformation and Branch Motion

Since several deformations need to be carried out for each vertex, the vertices are stored in object coordinates and the deformation, i.e., the offset, tangent and normal transformations shown in Section 4.4.3 are expressed in terms of the branch coordinate frame vectors, thus avoiding a full matrix transformation into the local coordinate system. The positional deformation of one level simplifies to

$$\vec{p_D} = \vec{p_o} - \frac{\vec{t}d_r(x) - \vec{r}u_r(x)}{s_r(x)} - \frac{\vec{t}d_s(x) - \vec{s}u_s(x)}{s_s(x)} \qquad (4.23)$$

with the length corrected x values

$$x_{D,r,s} = x - \frac{d_{r,s}(x)}{s_{r,s}(x)} \qquad (4.24)$$

the tangent and normal transformation results to

$$\vec{t_D} = \vec{t_o} + (u'_r(x_{D,r})\vec{r} + u'_s(x_{D,s})\vec{s})(\vec{t} \cdot \vec{t_o}) \qquad (4.25)$$
$$\vec{n_D} = \vec{n_o} - (u'_r(x_{D,r})(\vec{r} \cdot \vec{n_o}) + u'_s(x_{D,s})(\vec{s} \cdot \vec{n_o}))\vec{t} \qquad (4.26)$$

This deformation is executed down the tree hierarchy, starting from the trunk until the level of the vertex is reached (i.e., as long as $x = \vec{w}_i \neq 0$). For the first iteration, $\vec{p_o}, \vec{t_o}, \vec{n_o}$ are the original position, tangent and normal in object space, for all further iterations they are set to $\vec{p_D}, \vec{t_D}, \vec{n_D}$ from the previous iteration. Analogue to the tangents, all involved child branch local frames under the current hierarchy level need to be transformed according to equation (4.25). Normals and tangents need to be normalized only after all deformations have been carried out because they are always reprojected into the current coordinate system.

As shown in Section 4.3, the vertex needs access to the branch parameters of all its parent branches to execute these transformations. In particular, the

4.7. LEAVES

Per hierarchy level	motion texture
Per branch	$c_2, c_4, L, \vec{t}, \vec{r}, \vec{s}, \vec{m}$, motion tex. index
Per vertex	$\vec{w}$, branch index

Table 4.2: Data required to deform a vertex and associated normal and tangent. The per branch data is accessed through the branch index and the motion textures are accessed through the motion texture index.

terms dependent on x (e.g., $u_{r,s}(x)$) are simple polynomials in x with parameters c_2, c_4 (equation (4.8)). Denormalization also requires the length L, and motion is accounted for by looking up $A_{r,s}$ from a motion texture (equation (4.12)). The branch parameters and data of the whole tree are stored in a branch data texture, which the vertex can access based on its branch index, treating the texture as a data array accessible in the vertex shader. Each column of this floating point texture contains all the data of a branch, followed by the data of all parent branches. This means that some of the data is redundant, but this configuration facilitates caching accesses and speeds up the data retrieval considerably. Analogue to the branch index, every branch has a motion texture index and motion vector $\vec{m}$ for the texture lookups to obtain $A_{r,s}$ (used in the evaluation of $u_{r,s}$). Using a texture-based data representation has the advantage that low-level per-branch parameters such as α or L can be edited in real time by simply modifying the corresponding texels. Table 4.2 summarizes which variables are represented on which level.

4.7 Leaves

Leaves need to be treated slightly different from branches because they do not need complex deformation and their motion behavior is different. But a modified version of the previously shown set of methods can be applied to ensure full consistency of both branch and leaf animation. Also, the same means to derive the motion from physical properties is upheld.

4.7.1 Leaf Deformation

In the shown trees, leaves are represented as flat quads, though any geometric configuration can be chosen. Leaves are treated as part of the branch they are attached to and therefore inherit all deformations of their parent branches. Thus, a leaf vertex has the same data as a branch vertex of the branch it is attached to. Apart from the inherited branch deformations, an additional

CHAPTER 4. PHYSICALLY GUIDED ANIMATION OF TREES

animation is executed to perform the fluttering of leaves in the wind, modeled with a simplified version of the branch deformation, but with additional torsional motion.

For the local coordinate system, the tangent space $(\vec{t}_t, \vec{b}_t, \vec{n}_t)$ is used, so no additional data is needed if the leaves need a tangent space for shading. The UV coordinates of the vertices, denoted by u_t, v_t to avoid confusion, serve as local coordinates in this space, using a corrected coordinate $u'_t = (1 - u_t)/2$ along the $\vec{t}_t$ axis, assuming a centered stipe of the leaf (see Figure 4.15). The

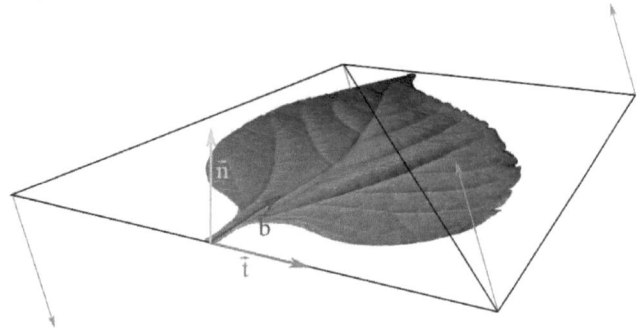

Figure 4.15: Additional torsional deformation preceding the transversal deformation for the leaves.

branch deformer from Section 4.4.3 is applied twice: for translational and for torsional flutter. For the translational flutter, the local coordinate axes $(\vec{t}, \vec{r}, \vec{s})$ are set to $(\vec{b}_t, \vec{n}_t, \vec{t}_t)$, so that v_t is used for x. For the torsional flutter, $(\vec{t}, \vec{r}, \vec{s})$ are set to $(\vec{t}_t, \vec{b}_t, \vec{n}_t)$, with the corrected u'_t used for x. The opposing signs of u'_t ensure the counter movement of opposing vertices to model the torsional deformation.

In both cases, equation (4.23) and (4.26) are executed to carry out the deformation. As opposed to branches, there is no need for a fully nonlinear deformation for leaves. As a simplification, a linear function $u^l(x) = A^l x$ is used for all evaluations of $u(x)$, where A^l determines the strength of the deformation from motion texture lookups.

4.7.2 Leaf Animation

Since leaves are lightweight and small, they can be treated as samplers of the turbulent wind field. To generate a wind field, motion textures that use only the wind spectrum $P'_w(f)$ as input (see Section 4.5.3) are calculated.

4.8. RESULTS

The spatial relation of leaves in gusts of wind causes leaves to behave in a coherent way if they are close together, i.e., nearby leaves should have similar amplitudes and frequencies, but not necessarily directions. This could be accounted for by creating a 3D turbulence field for each flutter direction and moving this field along the wind direction $\vec{W}$. However, 3D textures of sufficient resolution to transport high frequencies and to avoid periodicity would be too memory intensive.

Instead, there is a solution using three independent 2D motion textures. Each leaf vertex is projected onto the three different planes $x, y, z = 0$ in object space and noise values $A^p_{xy,xz,yz}$ are fetched from the three motion textures after offsetting the vertex position by $-\vec{W}(t)$ where t represents time to effectively move the wind field through the tree. Since the vertex moves through the wind field directly as opposed to the motion vector $\vec{m}$ of the branches, the three values are spatially correlated as desired. However, their frequency spectra are scaled by the projection of the wind vector on the coordinate planes. To avoid too strong distortions of the power spectrum, the 3 values are linearly blended in a way that the textures whose frequency is best preserved receives the largest weight:

$$A^l = A^p_{xy}(1 - \frac{|W_z|}{|\vec{W}|}) + A^p_{yz}(1 - \frac{|W_x|}{|\vec{W}|}) + A^p_{xz}(1 - \frac{|W_y|}{|\vec{W}|}). \qquad (4.27)$$

While linear trajectories in the resulting 3D turbulence field do not have the exact wind spectra, they are still consistent and spatially correlated. The same measures against periodicity should be taken for the wind vector as in Section 4.5.2. Figure 4.16 shows a visualization of the lookups for one leaf vertex. The three noise textures for the three axes of leaf deformation (Section 4.7.1) are stored in the 3 channels of an RGB texture. The texture resolution is chosen so that the minimum wavelength represented in the leaf motion textures is 4 times the maximum leaf size. This avoids too high spatial frequencies which could cause vertices of a single leaf to behave inconsistently. Nonetheless, each vertex of a leaf performs a slightly different movement, so the leaf itself does not stay flat. This adds complexity to the overall appearance by mimicking the complex behavior of leaves in wind compared to the rigid rotation of flat quads [87]. This becomes especially apparent if a specular shading model is used for the leaves.

4.8 Results

To validate the shown set of methods and to evaluate the performance, trees with about 75k vertices, resulting in 1,500 branches and around 10,000 leaves

CHAPTER 4. PHYSICALLY GUIDED ANIMATION OF TREES

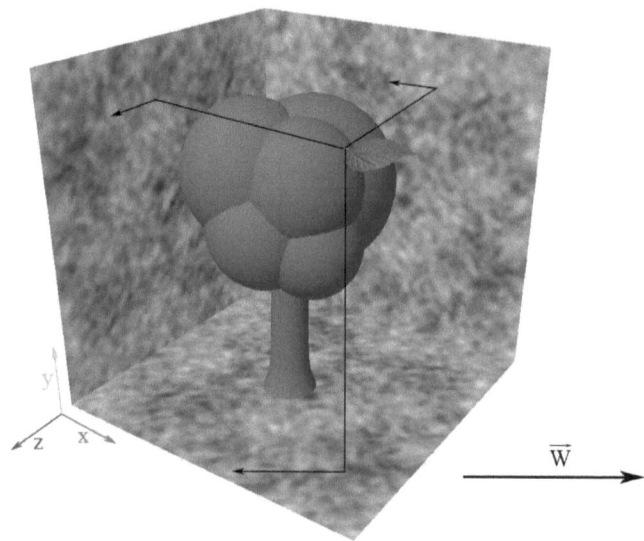

Figure 4.16: 3D turbulence field through averaged lookups of 3 motion textures.

divided into 4 hierarchy levels have been used. As input, the full branch hierarchy including the local coordinate systems and beam radii and lengths are needed. For the shown trees, this has been done with an extraction routine that analyzes the geometry of a given tree. In this way, for example Xfrog [28] trees can be animated without manual intervention. For trees with continuous geometry at the branch connection, one simply needs to determine $\vec{w}$ through the relative position to the local branch coordinate systems.

The implementation and performance measurements were done using DirectX 10 and a NVIDIA 8800 GTS graphics card with 512 MB RAM on a Pentium 4 (3.2 GHz). Since it is difficult to measure times separately due to the unified shader architecture and interleaving of texture lookups and ALU calculations of current graphics hardware, the results are compared to the non-animated tree, both shaded and unshaded. The shaded scene is rendered with a full HDR pipeline and dynamic filtered shadow maps and advanced shading algorithms, thus using the same resources as a modern computer game.

For the shaded and simplified case, the animation is executed two times due to the shadow mapping pass which is corrected for in the frame rate comparison in Table 4.3. In the shaded case, the animation time is longer

	static(fps)	animated(fps)	time(ms)
unshaded	299	290	0.104
shaded	56	48	1.49
simplified	56	52	0.68
4 trees	49	32	5.4

Table 4.3: Framerate comparison and animation-only time in the unshaded, shaded and full simplification and multiple trees case.

since fewer ALU units are available due to load balancing. It can be seen that the cost of animation (last column) of a full geometry tree is negligible compared to shading the tree, allowing the animation of several highly detailed trees with a cost that scales linearly with the number of trees. The proposed technique can be adapted to the animation and shading requirements of a scene. To further marginalize the performance impact, the length correction described in Section (4.4.2) can be omitted for small deflections in light wind. Additionally, by calculating only the positional animation and shading the tree in its undeformed state, the performance impact can be minimized (see Table 4.3) without loosing the overall appearance of the animation.

Though values for all parameters are derived from physical properties and measurements, these parameters can be tuned to match different needs or artists' visions and allow high-level as well as low-level controllability over the animation. A screenshot of the tuning setup can be seen in Figure 4.17. Every single parameter can be set or overridden in real time on a per-level, per-branch and per-vertex basis since previous states of the animation are never accessed.

4.9 Summary

The presented method allows efficiently animating highly detailed trees with a massive amount of branches and leaves in high quality. With the stochastic approach, there are no considerable costs and enough resources remain free for other calculations such as shading the tree or other parts of a natural scene. The novel beam and deformation model can calculate the bending of branches according to the basic physical properties of a tree accurately without the need to segment branches.

The shown set of methods are confined to a vertex shader using hierarchical vertex displacement, leveraging the performance of GPUs and also making it easy to integrate into existing frameworks.

The novelty about the deformation model is that it does not assume

CHAPTER 4. PHYSICALLY GUIDED ANIMATION OF TREES

Figure 4.17: Prototypical user interface to tune animation parameters.

a uniform beam but correctly takes the taper into account, which has an essential impact on the deflection behavior. Also, the length correction provides the means to counteract the stretching of the deflection without the need to precompute additional data. Additionally, due to the closed form of the deformation, normal and tangent transformations, essential for advanced shading techniques, are derived, which is usually not done for vertex displacement-based methods.

An advantage of the 2D motion textures is that an arbitrary number of aperiodic noise functions with a defined power spectrum can be generated, allowing memory reduction and a performance increase because only a texture lookup is needed to access the functions. Of course, as with every non-simulation method, trees cannot interact with the scene, though the animation could be overridden on any level by an explicit integration of the equations of motion.

In summary, the presented methods provide a simple and efficient way for high quality animation. There are no elaborate precomputations required and all parameters can be changed interactively, both on a high level such as the damping coefficient of a level, and on a very low level such as the physical properties of an individual branch.

5
Artists can color the sky red because they know it's blue. Those of us who aren't artists must color things the way they really are or people might think we're stupid.

Jules Feiffer

Skylight Models for SH-Lighting

5.1 Introduction

Achieving dynamic global illumination in real-time graphics is a long standing problem and is a complete research area in itself in computer graphics. Many approaches have been proposed, though most of them are impractical in a real-world application due to high memory resources or very high computation costs. Many techniques that are in a practical range use a precomputation step. Unlike light mapping techniques, the light transfer is precomputed instead of the light itself. To do that, the transfer operator is projected into a basis that enables one to evaluate the transfer in real time. The first and up to now most used basis are the spherical harmonics (SH) basis functions. Performing a precomputed radiance transfer (PRT) using spherical harmonics for static scenes under low-frequency dynamic lighting environments was first proposed by Sloan et al. [92]. There is a plethora of publications that also use the SH basis to calculate more advanced effects such as specular reflections [52, 83] or dynamic diffuse interreflections [34] and shadows [83].

To reduce the dimensionality of the incident light, those techniques use environment maps instead of a fully three-dimensional representation. The environment lighting is projected into the SH basis to generate the information needed to calculate the resulting radiance transfer. By doing so, the only variance in lighting that can be achieved is through rotating the SH representation of the original environment lighting, because calculating the SH basis coefficients on the fly is very time consuming and introduces objectionable errors if undersampled. To avoid these problems, an accurate but still compact method to calculate the lighting SH coefficients for a parameterized lighting environment such as a skylight model is presented, which allows changing all parameters on a frame-by-frame basis, including the number of spherical harmonics bands.

The shown method is not limited to a particular skylight model, though

CHAPTER 5. SKYLIGHT MODELS FOR SH-LIGHTING

all data presented uses the Preetham skylight model, since the model can be displayed efficiently in real time [46] and is the most used model in real-time graphics. Using the presented method, full consistency and physical plausibility of the displayed sky and the used SH lighting coefficients can be achieved. The Preetham skylight model also delivers both realistic colors and dynamic range, capturing lighting influences of the sun halo, sky color and their intensity distribution. All of these effects can be captured when lighting a scene using spherical harmonics (see Figure 5.1).

Figure 5.1: Scene lit with daylight configuration.

5.2 Related Work

The first use of harmonics in the context of skylight models was proposed by Dobashi et al. [29]. He uses a discrete cosine basis to speed up the evaluation of a skylight model by determining the optimal number of basis functions and evaluating the tabulated weights to reconstruct the hemispherical function. This method is only tangentially related to the shown method since a discrete cosine basis is used to display the sky in contrast to a full SH representation that is evaluated in SH PRT.

5.2. RELATED WORK

A similar but much simpler approach compared to the shown method is to use analytically defined light sources such as directional lights or disk lights and to derive an explicit formula for their SH coefficients [42]. Of course, only functions that can be represented in this way are applicable, limiting the lighting to simple functions.

5.2.1 Spherical Harmonics Lighting

In spherical harmonics lighting, the radiance transfer from an environment to a surface or volume is precomputed as the weights $c_{l,m}$ of spherical harmonics basis functions. Taking advantage of their orthogonality, the radiance transfer is evaluated at runtime using the inner product of the spherical harmonics weights calculated from dynamic lighting environment weights and the precomputed weights on the surface or volume in real time. A detailed description of this approach is given in [92, 25] and a practical presentation of the method can be found in [42].

The shown method is concerned with the efficient reconstruction of a parameterized environment in its spherical harmonics representation in order to be able to change all parameters in real time.

5.2.2 Preetham Skylight Model

The Preetham skylight model [78] approximates the full spectrum daylight for various atmospheric conditions. It uses spectral calculations and the results are generated through fitted simulation data from Nishita et al. [69] as well as Perez et al. [80], is verified against standard literature from atmospheric science and therefore delivers realistic colors and dynamic range. The parameters for this model are the sun's angle to the zenith θ_S, azimuthal angle ϕ and angle from the zenith of the viewing direction θ and turbidity τ, which represents the cloudiness and haziness of the atmosphere. To simplify the solution, the angle γ between the solar and view direction is used (see Figure 5.2).

The parameter range of the turbidity is reduced to [2.5..6] since, as shown by Zotti et al. [107], values below 2.5 produce too high intensities at the horizon and the model is not usable for lighting below this parameter value. Since the skylight model is used for lighting through PRT rather than actually displaying a sky, its SH representation is considered as the ground truth. This is because the maximum frequency that can be represented is not limited by the Preetham skylight model or the shown method, but by the number of bands that are used to dynamically light a scene.

CHAPTER 5. SKYLIGHT MODELS FOR SH-LIGHTING

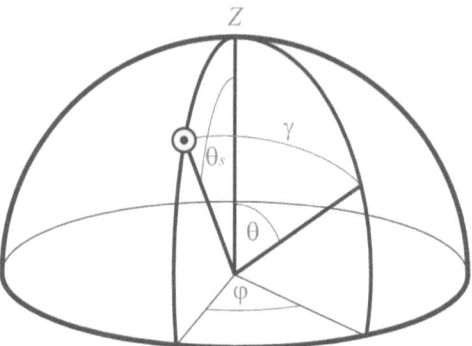

Figure 5.2: Coordinates used in the Preetham model: θ_S solar angle from zenith, ϕ θ angles of view direction, γ angle between solar and view direction. (picture: [106])

5.3 Dynamic Skylight

The goal is to represent the spherical harmonic weights as functions of the skylight's model parameters: $c_{l,m}(\theta_S, \phi, \tau)$. A naive solution is a full tabulation in all three parameters. However, this would needlessly waste memory as this three-dimensional function would need a high resolution to avoid interpolation artifacts. Also, memory can be an important issue on hardware platforms such as consoles or mobile devices. Furthermore, it is difficult to maintain a low error over a large dynamic range, which is important since postprocessing operators such as tone mapping and multi-bounce PRT strongly modulate intensity values, so no assumptions about the needed accuracy can be made.

The azimuthal angle ϕ can be eliminated from the preprocessing calculations by exploiting the fact that it represents a z-rotation around the zenith of the hemispherical function. Since a rotation is a linear transformation in spherical harmonics, the evaluation of ϕ can be deferred to the very end of the calculations, effectively reducing the needed parameter space of the preprocess to the two dimensions (θ_S, τ) without introducing an error. For these remaining two parameters, the key observation is that all SH weights show a largely polynomial behavior in (θ, τ). Therefore the SH-weights can be well compressed by performing a two-dimensional polynomial least squares fit in θ and τ, making a very fast real-time reconstruction possible. Other bases such as a discrete Fourier basis can also be used but showed higher errors with the same number of coefficients. The reason for that is that no basis

5.3. DYNAMIC SKYLIGHT

function correlations such as orthogonality or analytic convolution equations are needed and a direct fit of a polynome delivers the smallest error for a fixed set of coefficients.

5.3.1 Polynomial Fitting and Reconstruction

Each SH weight, treating the three color channels separately, is represented as a polynome of degree (d_i, d_j) with coefficients $(p_{l,m})_{i,j}$:

$$c_{l,m}(\theta_S, \tau) = P_{l,m}(\theta_S, \tau) = \sum_{i,j}(p_{l,m})_{i,j}\theta_S^i\tau^j, \ i = 0..d_i, \ j = 0..d_j \quad (5.1)$$

To determine the coefficients, all SH weights $c_{l,m}$ are calculated on a dense grid in (θ_S, τ). To avoid any errors and because the calculation time for the preprocess is not important, a grid with 500 samples in both θ_S and τ was chosen. The convolution of each SH basis function with the skylight function at every grid point in parameter space is generated by sampling until the result converges. This way no error is introduced in the preprocessing. This approach effectively treats the skylight model as a black box, so any parameterizable signal can be used. This data is then used for a polynomial least squares fit in (θ_S, τ), resulting in the polynomial coefficient matrix [8] $(p_{l,m})_{i,j}$ for each SH weight $c_{l,m}$. As the skylight model is sampled densely in the complete reduced parameter space and projected into the SH basis, this preprocess requires several hours (about 2.3 hours on a P4 3.2 GHz), but has to be done only once for each skylight model because all possible configurations of the model are used.

To reconstruct the SH weights $c_{l,m}$ in real time, the fact that the polynomial parameter matrix $(\theta_S^i\tau^j)_{i,j}$ for a given set of parameters (θ_S, τ) is the same for all SH weights, is exploited. Therefore, for each SH weight, this matrix is multiplied and summed component wise with $(p_{l,m})_{i,j}$ to evaluate equation (5.1) and obtain $c_{l,m}^{rec}(\theta, \tau) = P_{l,m}(\theta, \tau)$. The reconstruction is required only once per frame and can therefore be easily carried out on the CPU.

After the reconstruction, the SH weights are rotated around the zenith to take the azimuthal angle ϕ into account. Fortunately, a z-rotation of a function represented in the SH basis is relatively simple and the rotation matrix does not need to be fully constructed since

$$c_{l,m}(\phi) = c_{l,m}\cos(\|m\|\phi) - \text{sgn}(m)c_{l,-m}\sin(\|m\|\phi), m \neq 0 \quad (5.2)$$

implicitly rotates the weights [52], only correlating $c_{l,m}$ with its counterpart $c_{l,-m}$. The zonal harmonics $(m = 0)$ weights are excluded because they are

CHAPTER 5. SKYLIGHT MODELS FOR SH-LIGHTING

symmetric along the z-axis and do not need to be modified. Since the rotation is analytic, no error is introduced through the ϕ-rotation.

5.3.2 Error Measurement

To measure the resulting error of the reconstruction, it has to be taken into account that the reconstructed signal is used in an inner product with the vector of surface SH weights, thus adding up the error contributions of each SH weight $c_{l,m}^{rec}$. Usually 4 to 5 bands are used for SH PRT, therefore allowing only very small individual errors in the reconstruction of each $c_{l,m}^{rec}$.

Since the surface weights are not known and vary over their complete intensity domain in a standard scene, the ΔL^∞ and ΔL^2 norms related to the minimum intensity $L_{\min}$ of the original data give a relative upper bound of the maximum (ΔL^∞) and mean (ΔL^2) error for each parameter set:

$$E_{\max}^u(\theta, \tau) = \frac{1}{L_{\min}} \sum_{l,m} \| c_{l,m}^{rec} - c_{l,m} \| \tag{5.3}$$

and respectively

$$E_{\mathrm{mean}}^u(\theta, \tau) = \frac{1}{L_{\min}} \sqrt{\sum_{l,m} (c_{l,m}^{rec} - c_{l,m})^2} \;. \tag{5.4}$$

Considering normalized surface SH weights, equations (5.3) and (5.4) are overestimates since a surface point never sees the whole environment. The error estimates are correct only for an unoccluded volume point which only occurs in the most simple scenes.

The maximum number of SH bands to be considered in the error measurements was chosen to be $N_{max} = 7$, which lies well above the number of bands commonly used. By fitting a polynomial with degree $d_i = 13$ in θ_S and degree $d_j = 7$ in τ, the highest mean error drops below 1.5% for 7 bands, introducing virtually no error ($E_{\mathrm{mean}}^u < 0.005\%$) up to 5 bands, ensuring an accurate reconstruction over the complete parameter range. A comparison of the overall worst case reconstruction can be seen in Figure 5.3. Figure 5.4 shows the highest upper bound error of the complete parameter range dependent on the number of bands used. In the unlikely case that higher band numbers are required, simply using a polynomial of higher degree decreases the error.

5.3.3 Gibbs Phenomenon Suppression

Skylight models are only defined on a hemisphere, whereas spherical harmonics are defined on the complete unit sphere. Since there is no information

5.3. DYNAMIC SKYLIGHT

Figure 5.3: Worst case reconstruction ($N = 7$, $\theta = \pi/2, \tau = 6$) with the correct signal (top), the reconstructed signal (center) and the difference (bottom).

given below the horizon, a jump discontinuity occurs because the lower hemisphere is not defined by the model. As in every finite frequency extension of a discontinuity, the Gibbs phenomenon [40] appears and causes severe ringing in the lower hemisphere. There are ways to reconstruct a spherical harmonics signal without ringing [38], but another basis change into Gegenbauer polynomials is required, which is infeasible for spherical harmonics lighting. The signal is used in an inner product and not to reconstruct the spatial signal as would be needed to display the sky.

In this special case, a domain specific solution can be applied since the discontinuity is not dependent on ϕ and is therefore separated in θ, only affecting the zonal harmonics ($m = 0$). Therefore, to suppress the ringing artifacts from the horizon, only the zonal harmonics are filtered with

$$c'_{l,0} = c_{l,0} \operatorname{sinc}(\frac{\pi l}{N}), \tag{5.5}$$

which is equivalent to a one-dimensional box filter in θ [7]. This causes a slight smoothing in θ but does not change the general appearance. Also, the weights are filtered only where necessary, keeping all vertical frequencies in

CHAPTER 5. SKYLIGHT MODELS FOR SH-LIGHTING

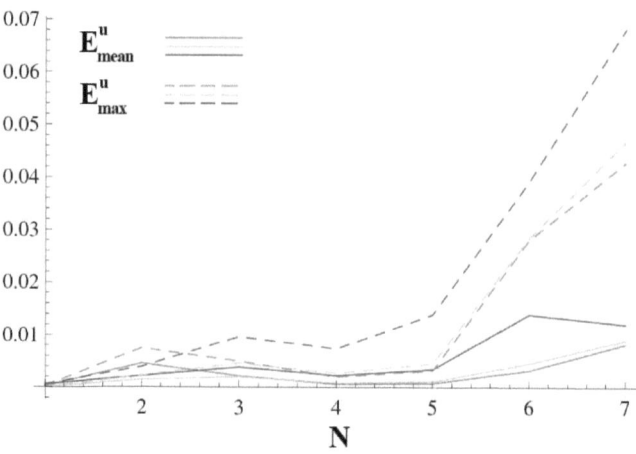

Figure 5.4: Highest upper bound mean and maximal relative error dependent on the number of bands N used of all color channels.

their original configuration. The ringing artifacts in the lower hemisphere are strongly reduced without introducing significant smoothing, leaving only slight artifacts from non-zonal harmonic contributions as seen in Figure 5.5.

Usually, the number of bands N used for PRT is fixed, allowing to prescale the zonal harmonics polynomial coefficient matrices $(p_{l,0})_{i,j}$ since equation (5.5) only depends on N, thus further reducing the required calculation at evaluation time.

5.4 Results

The resulting memory footprint for the matrix arrays is very small. 131 kByte are needed for $N = 7$ bands, while a more realistic number of bands of $N = 4$ reduces this to 28 kByte with trichromatic representation of the signal. So even for a relatively high number of bands, the required memory is small enough to completely fit into the L2 or even L1 cache of any modern processor, facilitating a considerable speedup through cache accesses. The maximum computation time for 7 bands on a P4, 3.2 GHz was measured at about 80 microseconds. Both computation time and memory resources needed are negligible compared to any other part of a graphics pipeline because the computation has to be done only once per frame for a fully dynamic skylight.

5.5. SUMMARY

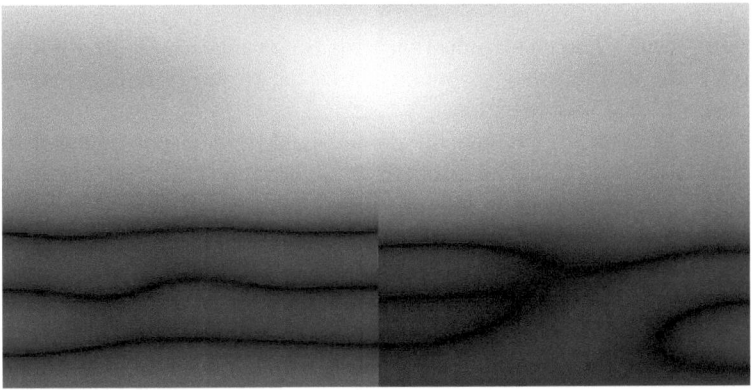

Figure 5.5: Original (left) and filtered (right) spherical harmonic reconstruction. The ringing artifacts from the horizon are strongly reduced.

As the full skylight model in its SH representation is calculated in the preprocess, the resulting data for the Preetham skylight model is published at [5] as C-arrays in conjunction with a full implementation of the reconstruction. The code is ready to be used in any spherical harmonics setup. A scene lit with SH PRT using $N = 5$ with different parameter sets can be seen in Figure 5.6.

Figure 5.6: Scene lit with SH PRT and the Preetham skylight at morning, midday and sunset.

5.5 Summary

The shown technique allows efficiently creating the lighting conditions for SH PRT while being negligible in both memory usage and calculation time. The error introduced through the polynomial fitting is insignificantly small and not perceivable even in the worst case. The method provides an easy to

CHAPTER 5. SKYLIGHT MODELS FOR SH-LIGHTING

implement way to generate physically correct SH lighting coefficients for any outdoor scene. The communication with the evaluation of SH PRT is only through the lighting weights, making it trivial to integrate skylights in any application that uses SH PRT.

Since the sun is a strong directional light that is not included in the skylight and can also not be properly integrated into SH PRT due to its inherently high frequencies in the directional lighting, SH PRT with a skylight naturally combines with standard shadow mapping. In the shown implementation, a Poisson filtered shadow map with 12 samples is overlayed with the SH PRT lighting to achieve fully dynamic outdoor lighting. To increase the realism, the directional lighting incorporates normal maps on all surfaces. Also, the color and intensity of the sun is modulated by the Preetham skylight model evaluated in the sun direction to guarantee a full consistency with the skylight. As the skylight model does not only produce correct colors but also a correct dynamic range, a Reinhard tone mapper [82] compresses the high dynamic range. This combination can provide a physically based and therefore realistic approach to light a natural scene dynamically. Figures 5.1 and 5.7 show a scene lit at different times of day with the given combination.

Figure 5.7: Scene lit at sunset. SH PRT using the Preetham model is combined with a directional light and Poisson filtered shadow mapping.

5.5. SUMMARY

An essential advantage is that only high level parameters such as sun direction or turbidity need to be controlled to achieve any daylight configuration without the need to set colors or intensities directly. Since SH basis functions are orthonormal, one can also overlay the reconstructed skylight weights with other lighting weights generated from a lower-hemisphere signal, either from an environment map of the lit scene or an isotropically colored lower hemisphere for example. This is not necessary for a scene with a terrain that occludes the lower hemisphere where the complete light transport is encoded correctly in the surface weights, but proved to be an easy way to generate a fully spherical lighting signal to light scenes which contain only one or a few objects.

Basic research is what I am doing when I don't know what I am doing.
Wernher von Braun

6
Summary and Conclusions

Real-time rendering and animation remains a challenging area of research, but significant progress has been made especially in the recent years. Though the fast paced development of more capable hardware allows increasingly more complex geometry and shading models to be rendered, the inherent complexity of vegetation still requires specialized techniques in order to achieve a convincing result. Most current applications and games that display vegetation still compromise strongly on the realistic appearance of vegetation as trees and grass are always part of a scene and enough resources need to be available for other entities. Although the presented work significantly improves on some problems one encounters while rendering or animating vegetation, a fully photo realistic tree or grass displayed interactively is still not achieved. A high-quality rendering of plants requires a considerable amount of resources as a plethora of effects such as the subsurface light transport through a leaf or the complex bending behavior of a branch combine to define the overall look of a plant.

As the technology advances, new possibilities will be available which will allow solving the problems with rendering and animating vegetation in a much more adaptive way, though the same paradigms as in the presented work still apply.

6.1 Key Contributions

Recent developments in GPU architecture allow performing a massive amount of calculations per frame. As of 2008, the TeraFLOP barrier has been breached and the graphics pipeline can handle arbitrary sequences of calculations. To make use of these capabilities, methods need to be able to be calculated fully on the GPU with the CPU involvement minimized. This approach has been taken in all the presented methods to fully leverage this advantage in both animating and rendering of vegetation.

CHAPTER 6. SUMMARY AND CONCLUSIONS

Also, the fact that a combination of techniques such as shadow mapping or dynamic lighting are usually used to display a scene has been taken into account. This requires the specialized vegetation rendering and animation methods to be able to be integrated with the more general techniques. In this thesis, the following contributions are made to these areas:

Grass Rendering. Grass, due to the massive amount of grass blades even in small patches of grass, make a naive geometric approach impractical for real-time rendering. A number of very different approaches have been proposed, depending on the grass properties as well as the viewers position. Due to the structure of grass, any polygon based approach results in a very high depth complexity. This problem has been remedied with the explicit ray tracing approach without compromising on the important perceptual effects such as parallax and correct occlusion, while delivering an easy yet effective way to animate the grass. Also, the rendering method is confined to a single fragment shader, treating grass as a volumetric material rather than geometry, which makes it easy to integrate into existing frameworks and to apply to a scene.

Leaf Rendering. Leaves exhibit a complex light transport, where the translucent part is dominated by subsurface scattering within a highly structured medium. The shown method to model translucency is the first physically based model for real-time rendering that includes essential effects such as self shadowing, spatially varying reflectance and thickness. The data acquisition does not require specialized hardware and can improve on the reflectance model of a leaf as well due to the high-resulution normal maps.

A big advantage is that the data can be trivially instanced to render a massive amount of leaves and can be combined with different geometric representations of leaves, which also facilitates the integration into existing applications.

Tree Animation. Animating highly detailed trees poses a number of challenges as the number of branches is in the thousands and the number of leaves in the ten thousands. The used branch deformation model takes all essential physical properties into account by using a structural mechanics model which also incorporates the taper of a branch. Also, the length correction provides the means to counteract the stretching of the deflection without the need to precompute additional data.

The spectral approach together with the 2D motion textures allows creating an arbitrary number of defined noise functions efficiently to get close to the results of a simulation without integrating the equations of motion or requiring elaborate precomputations.

Skylight Models for Spherical Harmonics Lighting. Traditional generation of lighting conditions for SH PRT are confined to using simple analytic functions or environment maps. The presented approach provides a way to efficiently generate the spherical harmonics lighting coefficients of a skylight model while keeping the memory foot-print and calculation resources at a minimum. The error introduced through the used polygonal fitting is insignificantly small and not perceivable even in the worst reconstruction case. As the Preetham skylight model is the most used in real-time graphics, the method has been validated using this model. Through defining the skylight model parameters such as sun direction and turbidity, any daylight configuration can be easily achieved in a spherical harmonics lighting context.

6.2 Research Outlook

The future of real-time vegetation rendering and animation lies in the new capabilities that future hardware can provide. Although current hardware (as of 2008) already has the possibility to create geometry on hardware, it is not yet usable for a full scene generation of grass and trees on the fly due to the complexity of the generation process. By generating only representations that are fully adapted to the current viewpoint, both rendering and animation can be adapted to the viewpoint as well.

Though being a more general problem, real-time global illumination within plants is a hard problem as many assumptions and simplifications do not work in the context of vegetation due to the fractal structure and non-coherent surfaces within plants. Considering a forest for example, most of the light is reflected or transmitted by leaves, so an accurate modeling of this lighting condition requires indirect illumination methods.

Recently developed techniques such as patch based ambient occlusion [48] or screen space ambient occlusion [58] are very successful for standard geometric objects but prove to be quite inefficient for vegetation due to the inherent depth complexity and incoherent surfaces. Also, a light-leaf interaction model that can be incorporated with global illumination algorithms is needed for a fully correct solution. As shown, it is important to include the full structure of a leaf to achieve convincing results.

CHAPTER 6. SUMMARY AND CONCLUSIONS

Concerning animation, hybrid approaches may be the most successful approach to incorporate interaction of vegetation with other parts of of the scene. As shown, it is not necessary to fully simulate the wind-vegetation interaction. By superimposing a stochastic approach with a simulation where necessary, the resources of a full simulation are not needed while partial interaction could be modeled. For example, while the animation of a tree is driven by a spectral model, a few branches that are interacting with objects in a scene could be explicitly integrated to model the correct response, blending back to the stochastic approach after the interaction is finished.

6.3 Conclusion

It seems that natural scenes, be it a tropical island, the jungle or ancient forests on alien planets, have a strong appeal as a setting for games. Only few games avoid vegetation completely, others are fully based in a natural setting with an abundance of vegetation. Plants will always be a part of almost every real-world scene and therefore form an essential part of computer graphics. As the technology progresses, new possibilities will be available to increase the quality of all aspects, but specialized techniques still will be necessary to optimize the calculations.

Significant advances have been made, but a fully photo-realistic real-time display of plants down to the last detail is still far ahead. Nonetheless, state-of-the-art methods as presented in this thesis can provide the visual complexity in both appearance and animation needed to render many forms of vegetation in a convincing and faithful way.

Appendix A

HLSL implementation of the grass rendering method shown in Chapter 2.

```hlsl
void BillboardGrass_VP(
    float4 position : POSITION,
    float3 normal   : NORMAL,
    float2 texCoord  : TEXCOORD0,
    float2 texCoord2 : TEXCOORD1,
    float3 tangent   : TEXCOORD2,
    float4 vertColor : COLOR,

    out float4 oVertColor     : COLOR,
    out float2 otexCoord      : TEXCOORD0,
    out float2 otexCoord2     : TEXCOORD1,
    out float4 oPosition      : POSITION,
    out float3 oEyeDirTex     : TEXCOORD2,
    out float4 oPositionView  : TEXCOORD3,

    uniform float4x4 worldViewProj,
    uniform float3 eyePositionO,
    uniform float time
)
{
    oPosition = mul(worldViewProj, position);
    oPositionView = oPosition;
    otexCoord = texCoord;
    otexCoord2 = float2((texCoord2.x+time*0.2)/2,(texCoord2.y+time*0.2)/2);
    oVertColor = vertColor;

    float3 eyeDirO = -(eyePositionO-position) ; //eye vector object space
    float3 binormal = cross(tangent,normal);
    float3x3 TBNMatrix = float3x3(normalize(tangent),
                                  normalize(binormal),
                                  normalize(normal));

    oEyeDirTex = normalize(mul(TBNMatrix,eyeDirO));
}

#define MAX_RAYDEPTH 5
#define PLANE_NUM 16.0 //Defines the density of the grid per UV patch.
#define PLANE_NUM_INV (1.0/PLANE_NUM)
#define PLANE_NUM_INV_DIV2 (PLANE_NUM_INV/2)
#define GRASS_SLICE_NUM 8
#define GRASS_SLICE_NUM_INV (1.0/GRASS_SLICE_NUM)
//Defines the number of grass billboards/slices inside the grass texture,
//is used for modding/correcting the texture lookups
//to adress all the grass slices.
#define GRASSDEPTH GRASS_SLICE_NUM_INV
#define GRASS_SLICE_NUM_INV_DIV2 (GRASS_SLICE_NUM_INV/2)
//Grassdepth can be set independently, here it is derived from the number
//of slices to avoid texture stretching, provided the uv
//coordinates do not stretch the texture.
#define PREMULT (GRASS_SLICE_NUM_INV*PLANE_NUM)

void BillboardGrass_PS(
    in float4 vertColor    : COLOR,
    in float2 texCoord     : TEXCOORD0,
    in float2 texCoord2    : TEXCOORD1,
    in float3 eyeDirTex    : TEXCOORD2,
    in float4 positionView : TEXCOORD3,

    out float4 color : COLOR,
    out float depth  : DEPTH,

    uniform float4x4 worldViewProj,
    uniform sampler2D grassblades,
    uniform sampler2D ground,
    uniform sampler2D windnoise
)
{
    float2 plane_offset = float2(0.0,0.0);
    color = float4(0.0,0.0,0.0,0.0);

    int hitcount;
    float3 rayEntry = float3(texCoord.xy,0.0);
    //everything that is not dependent on the if cases is precomputed
```

105

```
float2 sign = float2(sign(eyeDirTex.x),sign(eyeDirTex.y));
float2 plane_correct = float2((sign.x+1)*GRASS_SLICE_NUM_INV_DIV2,
                              (sign.y+1)*GRASS_SLICE_NUM_INV_DIV2);
//plane_correct is used to make sure that the same grass is seen from both sides.
float2 planemod = float2(floor(rayEntry.x*PLANE_NUM)/PLANE_NUM,
                         floor(rayEntry.y*PLANE_NUM)/PLANE_NUM);
float2 pre_dir_correct = float2((sign.x+1)*PLANE_NUM_INV_DIV2,
                                (sign.y+1)*PLANE_NUM_INV_DIV2);

//This is used to extract a z value from the calculations.
float zOffset = 0.0;
bool zflag = 1;


for(hitcount =0; hitcount < MAX_RAYDEPTH % (MAX_RAYDEPTH+1); hitcount++)
{
    float2 dir_correct = float2(sign.x*plane_offset.x+pre_dir_correct.x,
                                sign.y*plane_offset.y+pre_dir_correct.y);
    float2 distance = float2 ((planemod.x + dir_correct.x - rayEntry.x)/(eyeDirTex.x),
                              (planemod.y + dir_correct.y - rayEntry.y)/(eyeDirTex.y));
    float3 rayHitpointX = rayEntry + eyeDirTex *distance.x;
    float3 rayHitpointY = rayEntry + eyeDirTex *distance.y;

    //Check if we hit the ground
    if ((rayHitpointX.z <= -GRASSDEPTH)&& (rayHitpointY.z <= -GRASSDEPTH))
    {
        float distanceZ = (-GRASSDEPTH)/eyeDirTex.z; // rayEntry.z is 0.0 anyway
        float3 rayHitpointZ = rayEntry + eyeDirTex *distanceZ;
        float2 orthoLookupZ = float2(rayHitpointZ.x,rayHitpointZ.y);

        color = (color)+ ((1.0-color.w) * tex2D(ground,orthoLookupZ));
        if(zflag ==1) zOffset = distanceZ;
        zflag = 0; // Set flag to 0 so we know that we have a correct z value
    }
    else
    {
        float2 orthoLookup;
        if(distance.x <= distance.y)
        {
            float4 windX = (tex2D(windnoise,texCoord2+rayHitpointX.xy/8)-0.5)/2;
            // The /8 maps the texcoord lookup to world coordinates

            //The correct grass texture lookup is calculated
            float lookupX =
            -(rayHitpointX.z+(planemod.x+sign.x*plane_offset.x)*PREMULT)-plane_correct.x;
            orthoLookup =
            float2(rayHitpointX.y+windX.x*(GRASSDEPTH+rayHitpointX.z),lookupX);

            plane_offset.x += PLANE_NUM_INV;
            if(zflag ==1) zOffset = distance.x;
        }
        else {
            float4 windY = (tex2D(windnoise,texCoord2+rayHitpointY.xy/8)-0.5)/2;
            float lookupY =
            -(rayHitpointY.z+(planemod.y+sign.y*plane_offset.y)*PREMULT)-plane_correct.y;
            orthoLookup =
            float2(rayHitpointY.x+windY.y*(GRASSDEPTH+rayHitpointY.z) ,lookupY);
            plane_offset.y += PLANE_NUM_INV;
            if(zflag ==1) zOffset = distance.y;

        }
        color += (1.0-color.w)*tex2D(grassblades,orthoLookup);
        //If the alpha is greater than 0.49, we take the current value as z
        if(color.w >= 0.49){zflag = 0;}
    }
}
//Blend in a background color ir there is some transparency left.
color += (1.0-color.w)*float4(0.32156,0.513725,0.0941176,1.0);
color.xyz *= (vertColor.xyz);
positionView += mul(worldViewProj,eyeDirTex.xzy*zOffset);
depth = positionView.z/positionView.w;

}
```

List of Figures

2.1 A screenshot of the game Crysis using billboards for vegetation rendering. (picture: [3]) 8
2.2 Grass ray traced through volumetric texels. (picture: [67]) . . 10
2.3 Shells over a terrain and the resulting grass. (pictures: [9]) . . 11
2.4 Terrain with shell based grass. (picture: [10]) 11
2.5 BTF based grass. (pictures: [86]) 12
2.6 Shadow mask of a grass blade (left) and resulting shadows (right). (pictures: [15]) 14
2.7 Different LODs of grass. (picture: [15]) 15
2.8 Meadow rendered with the method proposed by Boulanger [15]. 16
2.9 A quad patch (wireframe overlay) rendered with fully opaque textures. The grid structure is generated in the fragment shader. 17
2.10 A grass data set consisting of grass blades (left), a ground texture (right) and a fully opaque grass slice (bottom). 18
2.11 A ray is cast from the viewing point through a grid of grass slices. 19
2.12 A quad patch rendered with the data set of Figure 2.10. The grid structure is apparent at perpendicular angles but vanishes at more grazing angles. 21
2.13 A quad patch with the same data set as in Figure 2.12, but with an additional horizontal plane at half the ground depth. The grid structure is not dominant even at perpendicular angles. 22
2.14 A grass patch with (left) and without (right) correct visibility. 23
2.15 A terrain textured with animated grass with moderate grass density and height. 25
2.16 A terrain textured with short, dense grass. 26

3.1 Leaves in sunlight. 30
3.2 A linear light source (LLS) used to measure reflectometry. (picture: [37]) 32

3.3 Front lit (left) and back lit (right) rendered with the model proposed by Baranoski et al. [12]. 33
3.4 Leaves rendered with the method proposed by Wang et al. [99]. 34
3.5 Front and back, front lit (left pictures) and back lit (right pictures). (pictures: [30]) 35
3.6 Plant rendered with single scattering according to Franzke et al. [35]. 36
3.7 Schematics of the acquisition setup and a close up of the fixing frame. For the 3D scan, the 3D scanner replaces the diffuser. . 38
3.8 The scanned geometry, normal-mapped simplified geometry and the normal map on a quad patch. The highlights have been exaggerated for visualization purposes. 39
3.9 A complete data set of a leaf, consisting of albedo (left), translucency (middle) and normal map (right) for both sides and a thickness map (bottom). 40
3.10 Quad patches shaded with highly specular (top) and almost diffuse (bottom) reflectance, and with a directional light at steep (left) and grazing angle (right). 42
3.11 Physically based leaf translucency (top) with light at different angles from steep (left) to grazing angles (right) in comparison to the standard diffuse translucency model (bottom). 43
3.12 Fluence field defined by the multi dipole configuration. Green are positive, red are negative values. 47
3.13 Transmittance at different thickness d and distance r for a fixed set of physical properties. 48
3.14 The 3 vectors that define the Half Life 2 basis. The colors correspond to their coefficient channel. 51
3.15 The Half Life 2 basis functions. Red are positive and blue are negative values. 52
3.16 The normal map, height map, and the resulting HL2 coefficient map. 54
3.17 Leaf on a tree showing fully consistent reflectance and translucency at grazing light directions. 56
3.18 A tree featuring physically based translucency. 57
3.19 Error histogram of the relative signal reconstruction error for 3 light directions. 58
3.20 Leaf shaded with multi-dipole model L_t (left) and the reconstructed translucency $L_{t,rec}$ (right) at a light angle of $\pi/8$. . . 59

3.21 A direct comparison of the standard method (left) to the shown method (right) shows improved structure due to normal mapping, and the physically based appearance of translucency in the leaves. 60

4.1 Detailed animated tree. 63
4.2 Fully simulated tree with fluid dynamics simulated wind. (picture: [6]) 64
4.3 Frames of an animation of a small tree animated with precalculated modal shapes. (picture: [95]) 66
4.4 Frames of an animation of a palm tree using a procedural per vertex animation. (picture: [93]) 67
4.5 Frames of an animation of a small tree using a procedural approach. (picture: [87]) 67
4.6 $\vec{w}$ distribution of branches in a tree. 68
4.7 Beam model used to calculate the deflection of branches. . . . 70
4.8 Deflection for different taper ratios. With decreasing taper ratio, the beam deflection increases due to the thinning of the branch. 71
4.9 Geometry of the length correction. (parameter x omitted for clarity). 72
4.10 Strongly deflected and length corrected beam. 73
4.11 Local coordinates for a branch. 74
4.12 Branch including sub-branches in the undeformed (left) and a deformed (right) state. The sub-branches follow the deformation correctly. 75
4.13 Example wrapped trajectory through the motion texture (left) which results in a aperiodic signal with a defined spectrum (right). 79
4.14 Spectra and parts of the resulting textures for the damped (top) and the overdamped case (bottom). 81
4.15 Additional torsional deformation preceding the transversal deformation for the leaves. 84
4.16 3D turbulence field through averaged lookups of 3 motion textures. 86
4.17 Prototypical user interface to tune animation parameters. . . . 88

5.1 Scene lit with daylight configuration. 90
5.2 Coordinates used in the Preetham model: θ_S solar angle from zenith, ϕ θ angles of view direction, γ angle between solar and view direction. (picture: [106]) 92

109

5.3 Worst case reconstruction ($N = 7$, $\theta = \pi/2, \tau = 6$) with the correct signal (top), the reconstructed signal (center) and the difference (bottom)............................... 95

5.4 Highest upper bound mean and maximal relative error dependent on the number of bands N used of all color channels. . . 96

5.5 Original (left) and filtered (right) spherical harmonic reconstruction. The ringing artifacts from the horizon are strongly reduced. 97

5.6 Scene lit with SH PRT and the Preetham skylight at morning, midday and sunset. 97

5.7 Scene lit at sunset. SH PRT using the Preetham model is combined with a directional light and Poisson filtered shadow mapping. 98

List of Tables

2.1 Average frames per second for different hardware ans resolutions. 26

3.1 Parameters used for the calculation and precomputation of subsurface scattering. 55

4.1 Coefficients for equation (4.8) of different values of the taper ratio α. 72

4.2 Data required to deform a vertex and associated normal and tangent. The per branch data is accessed through the branch index and the motion textures are accessed through the motion texture index. 83

4.3 Framerate comparison and animation-only time in the unshaded, shaded and full simplification and multiple trees case. 87

Bibliography

[1] OGRE Graphics Engine
http://www.ogre3d.org.

[2] Geomagic Studio, Geomagic
http://www.geomagic.com.

[3] Crysis, 2006. Crytek
http://www.crytek.com.

[4] http://www.cg.tuwien.ac.at/research/publications/2007/Habel_2007_RTT/, 2007.

[5] http://www.cg.tuwien.ac.at/research/publications/2008/Habel_08_SSH/, 2008.

[6] Y. Akagi and K. Kitajima. Computer animation of swaying trees based on physical simulation. *Computers and Graphics*, 30(4):529–539, 2006.

[7] A. Antoniou. *Digital Filters, Analysis, Design, and Applications*. McGraw-Hill, New York, NY, USA, 1993.

[8] Kendall E. Atkins. *Numerical Analysis*. John Wiley and Sons, 1988.

[9] Brook Bakay and Wolfgang Heidrich. Real-time animated grass. In *Proceedings of Eurographics (short paper)*, 2002.

[10] Sven Banisch and Charles A. Wuthrich. Making grass and fur move. *Journal of WSCG*, 14(1-3):25–32, January 2006.

[11] G. Baranoski and J. Rokne. An Algorithmic Reflectance and Transmittance Model for Plant Tissue. *Computer Graphics Forum*, 16(3), 1997.

[12] G. Baranoski and J. Rokne. Efficiently simulating scattering of light by leaves. *The Visual Computer*, 17(8):491–505, 2001.

[13] K. E. Bisshopp and D. C. Drucker. Large deflection of cantilever beams. *Quarterly of applied Math*, 3(3):272–275, 1945.

[14] James F. Blinn. Models of light reflection for computer synthesized pictures. *SIGGRAPH Comput. Graph.*, 11(2):192–198, 1977.

[15] Kévin Boulanger, Sumanta Pattanaik, and Kadi Bouatouch. Rendering grass terrains in real-time with dynamic lighting. In *SIGGRAPH '06: ACM SIGGRAPH 2006 Sketches*, page 46, New York, NY, USA, 2006. ACM.

[16] L. Bousquet, S. Lacherade, S. Jacquemoud, and I. Moya. Leaf BRDF measurements and model for specular and diffuse components differentiation. *Remote Sensing of Environment*, 98:201–211, 2005.

[17] Antoine Bouthors, Eric Bruneton, Fabrice Neyret, and Nelson Max. Real-time subsurface scattering on the gpu. Technical report, INRIA, 2007.

[18] Yung-Yu Chuang, Dan B Goldman, Ke Colin Zheng, Brian Curless, David H. Salesin, and Richard Szeliski. Animating pictures with stochastic motion textures. *ACM Trans. Graph.*, 24(3):853–860, 2005.

[19] Kim D. Coder. Sway frequency in tree stems. *University Outreach Publication*, FOR00-24, 2000.

[20] Jonathan Cohen, Marc Olano, and Dinesh Manocha. Appearance-preserving simplification. In *SIGGRAPH '98: Proceedings of the 25th annual conference on Computer graphics and interactive techniques*, pages 115–122, New York, NY, USA, 1998. ACM Press.

[21] Michael F. Cohen, Jonathan Shade, Stefan Hiller, and Oliver Deussen. Wang tiles for image and texture generation. *ACM Transactions on Graphics*, 22(3):287–294, 2003.

[22] R. L. Cook and K. E. Torrance. A reflectance model for computer graphics. *ACM Trans. Graph.*, 1(1):7–24, 1982.

[23] Kristin J. Dana, Bram van Ginneken, Shree K. Nayar, and Jan J. Koenderink. Reflectance and texture of real-world surfaces. *ACM Trans. Graph.*, 18(1):1–34, 1999.

[24] Phillippe de Reffye, Claude Edelin, Jean Françon, Marc Jaeger, and Claude Puech. Plant models faithful to botanical structure and development. In *SIGGRAPH '88: Proceedings of the 15th annual conference*

on *Computer graphics and interactive techniques*, pages 151–158, New York, NY, USA, 1988. ACM.

[25] Kelly Dempski and Emmanuel Viale. *Advanced Lighting and Materials With Shaders*. Wordware Publishing Inc., Plano, TX, USA, 2004.

[26] Eugene d'Eon, David Luebke, and Eric Enderton. Efficient rendering of human skin. In *Rendering Techniques*, pages 147–157, Grenoble, France, 2007. Eurographics Association.

[27] Oliver Deussen, Pat Hanrahan, Bernd Lintermann, Radomír Měch, Matt Pharr, and Przemyslaw Prusinkiewicz. Realistic modeling and rendering of plant ecosystems. In *SIGGRAPH '98: Proceedings of the 25th annual conference on Computer graphics and interactive techniques*, pages 275–286, New York, NY, USA, 1998. ACM.

[28] Oliver Deussen and Bernd Lintermann. *Digital Design of Nature: Computer Generated Plants and Organics*. SpringerVerlag, 2004.

[29] Yoshinori Dobashi, Tomoyuki Nishita, Kazufumi Kaneda, and Hideo Yamashita. Fast display method of sky color using basis functions. In *Pacific Graphics '95*, 1995.

[30] Craig Donner and Henrik Wann Jensen. Light diffusion in multi-layered translucent materials. In *SIGGRAPH '05: ACM SIGGRAPH 2005 Papers*, pages 1032–1039, New York, NY, USA, 2005. ACM Press.

[31] Craig Donner and Henrik Wann Jensen. Rendering translucent materials using photon diffusion. In *SIGGRAPH '08: ACM SIGGRAPH 2008 classes*, pages 1–9, New York, NY, USA, 2008. ACM.

[32] David Luebke Eugene d'Eon. Advanced techniques for realistic real-time skin rendering. In Hubert Nguyen, editor, *GPU Gems 3*, chapter 14. Addison Wesley, July 2007.

[33] T. J. Farrell and M. S. Patterson. A diffusion theory model of spatially resolved, steady-state diffuse reflections for the noninvasive determination of tissue optical properties in vivo. *Med. Phys.*, 19:879–888, 1992.

[34] Kayvon Fatahalian, Advisor Doug, and L. James. Real-time global illumination of deformable objects, 2003.

[35] Oliver Franzke and Oliver Deussen. Rendering plant leaves faithfully. In *SIGGRAPH '03: ACM SIGGRAPH 2003 Sketches & Applications*, pages 1–1, New York, NY, USA, 2003. ACM Press.

[36] B. Ganapol, L. Johnson, P. Hammer, C. Hlavka, and D. Peterson. LEAFMOD: A new within-leaf radiative transfer model. *Remote Sensing of Environment*, 63:182–193, 1998.

[37] Andrew Gardner, Chris Tchou, Tim Hawkins, and Paul Debevec. Linear light source reflectometry. *ACM Trans. Graph.*, 22(3):749–758, 2003.

[38] Anne Gelb. The resolution of the Gibbs phenomenon for spherical harmonics. *Mathematics of Computation*, 66(218):699–717, 1997.

[39] Thomas Di Giacomo, Stéphane Capo, and François Faure. An interactive forest. In Marie-Paule Cani, Nadia Magnenat-Thalmann, and Daniel Thalmann, editors, *Eurographics Workshop on Computer Animation and Simulation (EGCAS)*, pages 65–74. Springer, sept. 2001. Manchester.

[40] J.W. Gibbs. Fourier series. *Nature*, 59:200, 1898.

[41] Y. Govaerts, S. J. M. Verstraete, and S. Ustin. Threedimensional radiation transfer modeling in a dycotyledon leaf. *Applied Optics*, 35(33):6585–6598, 1996.

[42] Robin Green. Spherical harmonic lighting: The gritty details. *Game Developers' Conference 2003*, 2003.

[43] William Van Haevre, Fabian Di Fiore, Philippe Bekaert, and Frank Van Reeth. A ray density estimation approach to take into account environment illumination in plant growth simulation. In *SCCG '04: Proceedings of the 20th spring conference on Computer graphics*, pages 121–131, New York, NY, USA, 2004. ACM.

[44] Pat Hanrahan and Wolfgang Krueger. Reflection from layered surfaces due to subsurface scattering. In *SIGGRAPH '93: Proceedings of the 20th annual conference on Computer graphics and interactive techniques*, pages 165–174, New York, NY, USA, 1993. ACM Press.

[45] Xuejun Hao and Amitabh Varshney. Real-time rendering of translucent meshes. *ACM Trans. Graph.*, 23(2):120–142, 2004.

[46] Naty Hoffman and Arcot J. Preetham. Real-time light-atmosphere interactions for outdoor scenes. *Graphics programming methods*, pages 337–352, 2003.

[47] J. Isidoro and D. Card. *Animated Grass with Pixel and Vertex Shader.* 2002.

[48] Yuntao Jia Jared Hoberock. *GPUGems: Programming Techniques, Tips, and Tricks for Real-Time Graphics*, chapter 12 High-Quality Ambient Occlusion. Addison-Wesley, 2004.

[49] Henrik Wann Jensen. A rapid hierarchical rendering technique for translucent materials. *ACM Transactions on Graphics*, 21:576–581, 2002.

[50] Henrik Wann Jensen, Stephen R. Marschner, Marc Levoy, and Pat Hanrahan. A practical model for subsurface light transport. In *SIGGRAPH '01: Proceedings of the 28th annual conference on Computer graphics and interactive techniques*, pages 511–518, New York, NY, USA, 2001. ACM Press.

[51] James T. Kajiya and Timothy L. Kay. Rendering fur with three dimensional textures. In *SIGGRAPH '89: Proceedings of the 16th annual conference on Computer graphics and interactive techniques*, pages 271–280, New York, NY, USA, 1989. ACM Press.

[52] Jan Kautz, Peter-Pike Sloan, and John Snyder. Fast, arbitrary brdf shading for low-frequency lighting using spherical harmonics. In *EGRW '02: Proceedings*, pages 291–296, Aire-la-Ville, Switzerland, Switzerland, 2002. Eurographics Association.

[53] Alexander Kharlamov. Next-generation speedtree rendering. In Hubert Nguyen, editor, *GPU Gems 3*, chapter 4. Addison Wesley, July 2007.

[54] Philippe Lacroute and Marc Levoy. Fast volume rendering using a shear-warp factorization of the viewing transformation. In *SIGGRAPH '94: Proceedings of the 21st annual conference on Computer graphics and interactive techniques*, pages 451–458, New York, NY, USA, 1994. ACM Press.

[55] Jerome E. Lengyel, Emil Praun, Adam Finkelstein, and Hugues Hoppe. Real-time fur over arbitrary surfaces. In *2001 ACM Symposium on Interactive 3D Graphics*, pages 227–232, March 2001.

[56] Jerome Edward Lengyel. Real-time hair. In *Proceedings of the Eurographics Workshop on Rendering Techniques 2000*, pages 243–256, London, UK, 2000. Springer-Verlag.

[57] X. Liu, P.-P. Sloan, H.-Y. Shum, and J. Snyder. All-Frequency Precomputed Radiance Transfer for Glossy Objects. *Proceedings Eurographics Symposium on Rendering*, 15:337–344, 2004.

[58] Miguel Sainz Louis Bavoil. Screen space ambient occlusion. *NVIDIA white paper*, 2008.

[59] Qinglin Ma, Akira Ishimaru, Phillip Phu, and Yasuo Kuga. Transmission, Reflection, and Depolariastion of an OPtical Wave For a Single Leaf. *IEEE Transactions on Geoscience and Remote Sensing*, 28(5):865–872, 1990.

[60] N. L. Max. Horizon mapping: shadows for bump-mapped surfaces. *The Visual Computer*, 4:109–117, 1988.

[61] G. McTaggert. Half-Life 2/Valve Source Shading. Technical report, Valve Corporation, 2004.

[62] Tom Mertens, Jan Kautz, Philippe Bekaert, Frank Van Reeth, and Hans-Peter Seidel. Efficient rendering of local subsurface scattering. In *PG '03: Proceedings of the 11th Pacific Conference on Computer Graphics and Applications*, page 51, Washington, DC, USA, 2003. IEEE Computer Society.

[63] Alexandre Meyer and Fabrice Neyret. Interactive volumetric textures. In George Drettakis and Nelson Max, editors, *Eurographics Rendering Workshop 1998*, pages 157–168, New York City, NY, July 1998. Eurographics, Springer Wien. ISBN 3-211-83213-0.

[64] G. Mller, J. Meseth, M. Sattler, Sarlette R., and R. Klein. Acquisition, Synthesis, and Rendering of Bidirectional Texture Functions. *Computer Graphics Forum*, 24(1):83–109, 2005.

[65] John R. Moore and Douglas A. Maguire. Natural sway frequencies and damping ratios of trees: concepts, review and synthesis of previous studies. *Trees*, 3(18):195203, 2004.

[66] R. A. Moss and W. E. Loomis. A Low Distortion Map Between Disk and Square. *Journal of the Iowa Agricultural Experiment Station*, J(2017):370–391, 1951.

[67] Fabrice Neyret. Modeling, animating, and rendering complex scenes using volumetric textures. *IEEE Transactions on Visualization and Computer Graphics*, 4(1):55–70, 1998.

[68] F. E. Nicodemus, J. C. Richmond, J. J. Hsia, I. W. Ginsberg, and T. Limperis. *Geometrical considerations and nomenclature for reflectance*. Jones and Bartlett Publishers, Inc., USA, 1977.

[69] Tomoyuki Nishita, Yoshinori Dobashi, and Eihachiro Nakamae. Display of clouds taking into account multiple anisotropic scattering and sky light. In *SIGGRAPH '96: Proceedings of the 23rd annual conference on Computer graphics and interactive techniques*, pages 379–386, New York, NY, USA, 1996. ACM.

[70] Manuel M. Oliveira and Fabio Policarpo. An efficient representation for surface details. *UFRGS Technical Report RP-351*, 2005.

[71] Peter E. Oppenheimer. Real time design and animation of fractal plants and trees. In *SIGGRAPH '86: Proceedings of the 13th annual conference on Computer graphics and interactive techniques*, pages 55–64, New York, NY, USA, 1986. ACM.

[72] M. S. Patterson, B. Chance, and B. C. Wilson. Time resolved reflectance and transmittance for the noninvasive measurement of tissue optical properties. *Appl. Opt.*, 28:2331–+, June 1989.

[73] Kurt Pelzer. *GPUGems: Programming Techniques, Tips, and Tricks for Real-Time Graphics*, chapter 7 Rendering Countless Blades of Waving Grass, pages 107–121. Addison-Wesley, 2004.

[74] Frank Perbet and Marie-Paule Cani. Animating prairies in real-time. In *SI3D '01: Proceedings of the 2001 symposium on Interactive 3D graphics*, pages 103–110, New York, NY, USA, 2001. ACM Press.

[75] Ken Perlin. An image synthesizer. In *SIGGRAPH '85: Proceedings of the 12th annual conference on Computer graphics and interactive techniques*, pages 287–296, New York, NY, USA, 1985. ACM Press.

[76] Fábio Policarpo, Manuel M. Oliveira, and Jo ao L. D. Comba. Real-time relief mapping on arbitrary polygonal surfaces. *ACM Trans. Graph.*, 24(3):935–935, 2005.

[77] Thomas Porter and Tom Duff. Compositing digital images. In *SIGGRAPH '84: Proceedings of the 11th annual conference on Computer graphics and interactive techniques*, pages 253–259, New York, NY, USA, 1984. ACM Press.

[78] A. J. Preetham, Peter Shirley, and Brian E. Smits. A practical analytic model for daylight. In Alyn Rockwood, editor, *Siggraph 1999, Computer Grahics Procedings*, pages 91–100, Los Angeles, 1999. Addison Wesley Longman.

[79] Przemyslaw Prusinkiewicz, Aristid Lindenmayer, and James Hanan. Development models of herbaceous plants for computer imagery purposes. *SIGGRAPH Comput. Graph.*, 22(4):141–150, 1988.

[80] J.R. Seals R. Perez and P.Ineichen. An all weather model for sky luminance distribution, 1993.

[81] William T. Reeves, David H. Salesin, and Robert L. Cook. Rendering antialiased shadows with depth maps. In *SIGGRAPH '87 Proceedings*, pages 283–291, New York, NY, USA, 1987. ACM Press.

[82] Erik Reinhard, Michael Stark, Peter Shirley, and James Ferwerda. Photographic tone reproduction for digital images. *ACM Trans. Graph.*, 21(3):267–276, 2002.

[83] Zhong Ren, Rui Wang, John Snyder, Kun Zhou, Xinguo Liu, Bo Sun, Peter-Pike Sloan, Hujun Bao, Qunsheng Peng, and Baining Guo. Realtime soft shadows in dynamic scenes using spherical harmonic exponentiation. In *SIGGRAPH '06: ACM SIGGRAPH 2006 Papers*, pages 977–986, New York, NY, USA, 2006. ACM.

[84] Tatsumi Sakaguchi and Jun Ohya. Modeling and animation of botanical trees for interactive virtual environments. In *VRST '99: Proceedings of the ACM symposium on Virtual reality software and technology*, pages 139–146, New York, NY, USA, 1999. ACM.

[85] Christophe Schlick. An inexpensive brdf model for physically-based rendering. *Computer Graphics Forum*, 13:233–246, 1994.

[86] Musawir A. Shah, Jaakko Kontinnen, and Sumanta Pattanaik. Realtime rendering of realistic-looking grass. In *GRAPHITE '05: Proceedings of the 3rd international conference on Computer graphics and interactive techniques in Australasia and South East Asia*, pages 77–82, New York, NY, USA, 2005. ACM Press.

[87] Ota Shin, Tadahiro Fujimoto, Machiko Tamura, Kazunobu Muraoka, Kunihiko Fujita, and Norishige Chiba. $1/f\beta$ noise-based real-time animation of trees swaying in wind fields. In *Computer Graphics International*, pages 52–59, 2003.

[88] Mikio Shinya and Alain Fournier. Stochastic motion-motion under the influence of wind. *Comput. Graph. Forum*, 11(3):119–128, 1992.

[89] Peter Shirley and Kenneth Chiu. A Low Distortion Map Between Disk and Square. *Journal of Graphics Tools*, 2(3):45–52, 1997.

[90] E. Simiu and R.H. Scanlan. *Wind Effects on Structures*. JohnWiley and Sons, 1986.

[91] Peter-Pike Sloan. Normal mapping for precomputed radiance transfer. In *SI3D '06: Proceedings of the 2006 symposium on Interactive 3D graphics and games*, pages 23–26, New York, NY, USA, 2006. ACM Press.

[92] Peter-Pike Sloan, Jan Kautz, and John Snyder. Precomputed radiance transfer for real-time rendering in dynamic, low-frequency lighting environments. In *SIGGRAPH '02 Proceedings*, pages 527–536, New York, NY, USA, 2002. ACM Press.

[93] Tiago Sousa. Vegetation procedural animation and shading in crysis. In Hubert Nguyen, editor, *GPU Gems 3*, chapter 16. Addison Wesley, July 2007.

[94] Jos Stam. Multiple scattering as a diffusion process. In *In Eurographics Rendering Workshop*, pages 41–50, 1995.

[95] Jos Stam. Stochastic dynamics: Simulating the effects of turbulence on flexible structures. *Computer Graphics Forum*, 16(3):C159–C164, 1997.

[96] Susan L. Ustin Stephane Jacquemoud. Leaf optical properties: A state of the art. In *8th Int. Symp. Physical Measurements & Signatures in Remote Sensing*, pages 223–232, 2001.

[97] Stephen Timoshenko, Donavan Young, and Weawer, Williams, Jr. *Vibration problems in engineering*. New-York : 1974, 1974.

[98] E.A. Walter-Shea, J.M. Norman, and B.L. Blad. Leaf bidirectional reflectance and transmittance in corn and soybean. *Remote Sensing of Environment*, 29:161–174, 1989.

[99] Lifeng Wang, Wenle Wang, Julie Dorsey, Xu Yang, Baining Guo, and Heung-Yeung Shum. Real-time rendering of plant leaves. In *SIGGRAPH '05: ACM SIGGRAPH 2005 Papers*, pages 712–719, New York, NY, USA, 2005. ACM Press.

[100] Rui Wang, John Tran, and David Luebke. All-frequency interactive relighting of translucent objects with single and multiple scattering. In *SIGGRAPH '05: ACM SIGGRAPH 2005 Papers*, pages 1202–1207, New York, NY, USA, 2005. ACM Press.

[101] Jakub Wejchert and David Haumann. Animation aerodynamics. In *SIGGRAPH '91: Proceedings of the 18th annual conference on Computer graphics and interactive techniques*, pages 19–22, New York, NY, USA, 1991. ACM.

[102] Fabian Di Fiore William Van Haevre and Frank Van Reeth. Physically-based driven tree animations. *Eurographics Workshop on Natural Phenomena*, pages 75–82, 2006.

[103] J.T. Woolley. Reflectance and Transmittance of Light by Leaves. *Plant Physiol.*, 47:656–662, 1971.

[104] Long Zhang, Chengfang Song, Qifeng Tan, Wei Chen, and Qunsheng Peng. Quasi-physical simulation of large-scale dynamic forest scenes. In *Computer Graphics International*, pages 735–742, 2006.

[105] Renaldas Zioma. Gpu-generated procedural wind animations for trees. In Hubert Nguyen, editor, *GPU Gems 3*, chapter 6. Addison Wesley, July 2007.

[106] Georg Zotti. *Computer Graphics in Historical and Modern Sky Observations*. PhD thesis, Institute of Computer Graphics and Algorithms, Vienna University of Technology, Favoritenstrasse 9-11/186, A-1040 Vienna, Austria, 2007.

[107] Georg Zotti, Alexander Wilkie, and Werner Purgathofer. A critical review of the preetham skylight model. In Vaclav Skala, editor, *WSCG ' 2007 Short Communications Proceedings I*, pages 23–30. University of West Bohemia, January 2007.

Die VDM Verlagsservicegesellschaft sucht für wissenschaftliche Verlage abgeschlossene und herausragende

Dissertationen, Habilitationen, Diplomarbeiten, Master Theses, Magisterarbeiten usw.

für die kostenlose Publikation als Fachbuch.

Sie verfügen über eine Arbeit, die hohen inhaltlichen und formalen Ansprüchen genügt, und haben Interesse an einer honorarvergüteten Publikation?

Dann senden Sie bitte erste Informationen über sich und Ihre Arbeit per Email an *info@vdm-vsg.de*.

Sie erhalten kurzfristig unser Feedback!

VDM Verlagsservicegesellschaft mbH
Dudweiler Landstr. 99
D - 66123 Saarbrücken

Telefon +49 681 3720 174
Fax   +49 681 3720 1749

www.vdm-vsg.de

Die VDM Verlagsservicegesellschaft mbH vertritt

Printed by Books on Demand GmbH, Norderstedt / Germany